WORKSHOP MANAGEMENT

WORKSHOP MANAGEMENT

A BEHAVIORAL AND

SYSTEMS APPROACH

By

DOUGLAS B. SIMPSON, Ph.D.

Associate Professor of Management
California State University
Fresno, California

and

PHILIP M. PODSAKOFF

Assistant Instructor
Indiana University
Bloomington, Indiana
Former Administrative Assistant
Goodwill Industries
San Joaquin Valley, Inc.
Stockton, California

CHARLES C THOMAS · PUBLISHER
Springfield · Illinois · U.S.A.

Published and Distributed Throughout the World by
CHARLES C THOMAS · PUBLISHER
Bannerstone House
301-327 East Lawrence Avenue, Springfield, Illinois, U.S.A.

© *1975, by* CHARLES C THOMAS · PUBLISHER
ISBN 0-398-3364-1
Library of Congress Catalog Card Number: 74-23140

*With THOMAS BOOKS careful attention is given to all details of
manufacturing and design. It is the Publisher's desire to present books that are
satisfactory as to their physical qualities and artistic possibilities and
appropriate for their particular use. THOMAS BOOKS will be true to those
laws of quality that assure a good name and good will.*

Printed in the United States of America
M-3

Library of Congress Cataloging in Publication Data

Simpson, Douglas B
  Workshop management.

  Includes bibliographical references and indexes.
  1. Sheltered workshops—Administration. I. Podsakoff, Philip M.,
joint author. II. Title.
[DNLM: 1. Handicapped. 2. Organization and administration. 3. Rehabilitation, Vocational. HD7256.U5 S61w]
HD7255.S55   658'.91'36285   74-23140
ISBN 0-398-03364-1

PREFACE

PRIVATE NONPROFIT WORKSHOPS for the physically and mentally handicapped and the socially maladjusted are gaining wide acceptance in the United States to meet the needs of an ever growing population:

> A little noted but significant development in the United States has been the growth of workshops for the handicapped. These are programs whose primary purpose is to provide work for handicapped and disadvantaged persons—work as a source of gainful employment or as a means of helping to solve human problems.[1]

While both authors feel that the development of these workshops should be construed as an increased social awareness and desire of our society to help its less fortunate members, we are equally aware of some of the problems that this development has caused in the administration of these facilities.

The genesis of this text is found in the concern shared by both authors as to the quality of managerial training presently provided those individuals filling administrative positions in such facilities. For, even though many of the staff positions (Occupational Therapist, Physical Therapist, and Rehabilitation Counselor, to name just a few) demand professional certificates in order to meet the job description requirements, the administrators of these facilities may not be required to possess any other special credentials, and in fact may be hired for no other reason than their innate ability to convince a board of directors that they have acquired knowledge of the rehabilitation process.

Undoubtedly, some individuals with the knowledge of this process are successful in establishing and developing good facilities programs, but an awareness has risen through the years that many private nonprofit workshops are having to survive on increasing amounts of "crisis" funds (*unanticipated* amounts of subsidization from local, state, or federal agencies)

---

[1] N. Nelson, *Workshops for the Handicapped in the United States: An Historical and Developmental Perspective* (Springfield, Charles C Thomas Publisher, 1971), p. vii.

because of the inability of their directors to effectively implement their programs. We feel this problem will take on new dimensions as workshops face greater contingencies and environmental constraints in trying to meet the ever expanding needs of the handicapped clients in their community. Nelson apparently shares our views:

> To extrapolate into the future requires assessing the past and the present as they affect future possibilities. Such an assessment can indicate how existing programs will be modified to meet new conditions or revised so that new and essentially different goals may be undertaken . . . . To move into a closer relationship with the outside world . . . and make a larger contribution to the solution of some of the country's most difficult problems, the workshop movement needs to take advantage of existing opportunities. Among major tasks that need doing are these:
> 1. Expand the perspective and add new dimensions to its scope and methodology.
> 2. Assume an advocate role as a spokesman for handicapped and disadvantaged persons.
> 3. Restate its concepts of dysfunction and its relationships towards handicapped and disadvantaged persons.
> 4. Develop a nonprofit work system.
> 5. Adjust work capability to the changes of the economic system.
> 6. Identify the organizational components of a work-oriented welfare program and the various skills needed by staff.
> 7. Adopt a new approach for new kinds of people.[2]

In order to accomplish these tasks, an improved relationship between the workshop practitioner and the various schools of business administration is needed. We are keenly aware of the inclusion of the administrative discipline into many areas outside of the "traditional boundaries" of the business school. However, bridging the worlds between the administrative discipline and the rehabilitation process is not easily accomplished:

> If the gulf between academics working in the management field and the practicing manager is to be bridged . . . and it must be bridged before the best use can be made of the facilities which are to be

---

[2] N. Nelson, *Workshops for the Handicapped in the United States: An Historical and Developmental Perspective,* pp. 387-407.

provided for management education . . . academics must realize that
in the present limited state of knowledge, management needs a system
of beliefs, and that the propagation of this system of beliefs is a
legitimate part of management education . . . and management must
recognize that a system of beliefs becomes less necessary as factual
knowledge is extended and must be prepared to modify and relin-
quish their assumptions as soon as evidence is produced to show that
they are no longer tenable.[3]

In light of recent empirical research, there is evidence that
many of the paradigms or management systems of values and
beliefs in rehabilitation must be changed. The traditional practice of placing individuals in administrative positions because of
their backgrounds in the "people services" field, is one of the
beliefs that must be critically examined in light of the attrition
rate and number of workshops that appear to be in the "crisis"
stage because of poor management direction.

Having experienced close contact with the administrative
processes of workshops, we feel it is necessary to pursue a
behavioral and systems approach to the aforementioned problems within that general framework. We are hopeful that this
will result in a better understanding of current empirical evidence, as well as application of theoretical concepts to the
workshop situation.

We look upon this task with interest and enthusiasm. For
though the importance of much of the research and theoretical
concepts to the managerial processes may have been revealed
more succinctly in other texts, we feel there is good reason to
relate these notions in such a way that workshop administrators
can see their application to their local situation. Though this
may be accomplished in part by encouraging managers to include themselves in classes on administration or getting involved in programs designed to improve administrative processes, it has been our experience that when most administrators
deal with a dynamic environment they feel that they have little
time to devote to anything other than the constant changes that
are taking place.

---

[3] J. Woodward, *Industrial Organization: Theory and Practice* (London, Oxford University Press, 1965), p. 257.

This text is designed to examine various administrative disciplines applied to the management of workshops for the practitioner. We have purposely limited the size and scope of this undertaking to enable the reader to get a feel of some of the foundations of current management practice. We feel this is necessary in order to provide understanding and to improve managerial proficiency. We are also hopeful that this text will serve as a benchmark from which others will be encouraged to expand and further develop managerial philosophies which are compatible with the ever changing needs of the handicapped of our nation.

INTRODUCTION

THERE ARE SOME INTERESTING, yet unfortunate, dichotomies present in the administration of the rehabilitation facilities commonly called workshops for the handicapped. For, even though these workshops have sophisticated methods of behavior modification, work simulation, and on-the-job training for their clients, they spend relatively little effort in the training and education of administrative staff members with respect to the subtleties of management and administration. We say unfortunate because it is these same determinants (management efficiency and effectiveness) which are of key importance to the success of such facilities.

Secondly, though many of these workshops establish as their primary goal the preparation of their clients for survival in the community without government aid or support, we find an increasing number of workshops asking for and receiving "crisis" funds (monies to meet unanticipated contingencies) from various local, state, and federal agencies in order to survive.

There are apparently three major reasons for the lack of management knowledge and skill which we believe are also the causal factors for the increase in "crisis" funding.

1. *Much of the administrative staffing of these facilities is done with individuals from the so-called "people service" educational backgrounds, rather than with individuals from the administrative or managerial discipline.*

In itself this practice may not seem too damaging until one realizes that a workshop, like any other organization that "sells" its goods or services to the community, must be run as a business in order to survive. If this situation is to occur, increased knowledge of the administrative and managerial processes must be introduced into the workshop situation.

We are aware of numerous attempts to alleviate the problems of an inexperienced administrative staff. Included in many of the degree credentials offered in Rehabilitation Counseling in the colleges and universities of our nation are courses designed specifically for the administration of workshops. In fact, some of these institutions of higher learning offer master's degrees in workshop administration.

The various Department of Rehabilitation agencies throughout California (with which we are most familiar) have sponsored numerous educational training workshops designed to provide free expert consultation for administrators and staff members in dealing with the administrative and managerial processes in workshops. These specialists may also be requested, free of charge, for on-site visits of a particular workshop.

Various other agencies and associations, including Cal-ARF (California Association for Rehabilitation Facilities), IARF (International Association for Rehabilitation Facilities), CARF (Commission for Accreditation of Rehabilitation Facilities), and GIA (Goodwill Industries of America), offer varying degrees of technical and administrative advice to workshop staff members in the form of regional specialists, journals, and various other publications directed at practitioners in the field.

We feel encouraged that each of these sources have accepted as one of their goals an increase in the administrative and management professionalism now present in the facilities area. Unfortunately, workshops do not survive in a stable environment, as anyone who is actively involved in workshop management will attest. Definitions of the handicapped are becoming broader, bringing forth new and different stresses which impact on the staffs; government regulations are becoming increasingly more stringent; workshop size has grown from tens and hundreds of clients to the thousands in some cases; and the contingencies of a changing environment have imposed heretofore unheard of dynamics in the workshop setting. There is little question then that the problems faced by the workshop today are in many cases not the same as those that will be faced next year, next month, or even next week! Because of this dynamism we sense a widening gap between the management knowledge acquired by staffs in workshops, and the new and ever-changing administrative problems they will face.

We are not suggesting nor advocating, however, the replacement of present staff members by individuals with greater depth in the managerial discipline, but rather we are advocating an increased level and sophistication in the training and education of administrative staff members in the future to deal with the "dynamics" of this highly volatile situation.

2. *There are few texts available that relate the administrative and managerial processes, organizational dynamics, or the selection and training of administrative staff, to such facilities.*

While we do not deny that there are many texts that deal with all of the above mentioned areas, there are few related specifically to the rehabilitation facilities area. In addition, within each of these areas we find diverse and often contradictory theories and empirical studies which lead to a confused and muddled situation for many practitioners. With many administrators and their staffs feeling that their primary purpose is rehabilitation, it is understandable why few want to trek into the management theory jungle.

Let us further submit that the process of rehabilitation cannot be accomplished by merely wanting it to be so. Someone, somehow, must acquire the resources which enable the program to function. How these resources are utilized (or managed) should be of great importance to many people. It seems only fair that the board of directors, the clients, the community, and other interested parties expect that the optimum resource allocation be attained in the accomplishment of workshop organizational goals. Therefore, it not only seems logical, but also imperative for truly successful workshops to accomplish the integration of the rehabilitation and administrative discipline.

3. *Workshops, because of their differences in functional organizational structures, have been considered by some practitioners to be too diverse to apply any one particular managerial style.*

We have all heard typical statements such as the following:

"Well, that may have worked for you, but our workshop is dealing with a different type of client, unlike any that anyone else is dealing with."

"In the southern part of the state, workshops have to perform differently because we deal with a stricter district administrator than you do."

"That doesn't apply to our workshop; we have other problems that no one else does."

We would be the first to agree that many facilities have their own special traits and unique problems which are peculiar only to themselves. But, at the same time, there are patterned similarities and differences that must be understood so that facilities can be analyzed effectively. Perrow seems to agree with this:

> All practitioners contend no two organizations are alike. Each insists that his organization is unique, indeed, even more unique than all other unique organizations . . . all organizations, like all organs and all cells, are indeed unique . . . . But there are enough systematic differences, and systematic similarities, to allow us to generalize . . . . Otherwise it would be impossible for us to use such terms as organizations, people, and cells. Without these generalizations, it would even be impossible for organizations to exist; organizations are based upon the assumption that an acceptable degree of standardization is possible, despite the irreducible uniqueness . . . . What we must discover are patterns of variation, which hold despite the uniqueness of markets, structure, personnel, history and environment and which provide fairly distinct types that can be used for analysis and prediction . . . . We must also discover the patterns that do obtain in market situations, structure and the rest . . . . To the manager, his organization is unique; but only by comparing it with the experience of other organizations can he learn much about it . . . .*

Having outlined the three problem areas concerning the lack of management knowledge and skills, what are the consequences the practitioner faces if these three areas are not successfully challenged and mastered? We believe that this will result in workshops becoming increasingly unable to accomplish the very things for their clients that they are attempting, namely, how to cope more effectively with their environment and to survive in it. In short, workshops face, and will continue to face in ever increasing instances, a serious question of their own legitimacy.

---

*An interesting treatment of technological variables in people-changing organizations along with many considerations of nonprofit organizations are developed in C. Perrow, *Organizational Analysis: A Sociological View* (Belmont, Brooks/Cole Publishing Company, 1970), p. 177.

Legitimization comes from such groups as consumers, suppliers, regulatory agencies, the investigating public, and the taxpayers—all a part of the organizations environment . . . . One of the implicit tasks of an organization then, is to establish the legitimacy of its output . . . . Legitimacy for nonprofit organizations is sometimes an even harder problem . . . agencies die more frequently than we realize because their legitimacy is questioned, and other agencies expend great resources to stay alive.[1]

It should appear self-evident that as consumers, suppliers, regulatory agencies, etc., look longer and deeper into the reasons, goals, and purposes of rehabilitation workshops, they will question to a greater degree some of the administrative and managerial processes that workshops utilize.

We are concerned about the questions of legitimacy that may be raised regarding many of the administrative processes. Therefore, some "method to the workshop's madness" must be provided within which the practitioner can relate various management processes to the field of rehabilitation workshops.

We feel that the most logical base from which to integrate the administrative and workshop processes lies with the incorporation of a behavioral and systems approach. This approach will enable us to look for the patterns of variation which are necessary in the analysis of similarities and differences between workshops.

In this approach we view the organization as an open system that acts and reacts interdependently with its environment. Understanding these interdependencies is crucial to the assessment of the managerial and behavioral actions within the organization.

In attempting to accomplish this integrative behavioral-systems approach, we have set some major goals and reservations which have guided us through the text:

1. *This text is designed to improve the workshop practitioner's ability to better conceptualize his problems in the administrative areas.*

One of the most difficult problems for any administrator is to distinguish the cause from its symptoms. Alternatives and the problem solution are much more easily accomplished if the

---

[1] Perrow, *Organizational Analysis: A Sociological View,* p. 177.

problem has been properly defined. The "problem of describing the problem" can frequently best be achieved by divorcing oneself from the superficialities that exist, and focusing on the problem from a higher level of abstraction or conceptualization:

> Some hold that conceptual study provides answers or solutions for the problems which practitioners encounter. But, questions must be asked before they can be answered, and asking meaningful questions is often as difficult as answering them . . . . This is especially true for administrators, who live and work among the phenomena of organizations. They are so much in and of the stream of happenings, so close to the events, that it is difficult for them to achieve a perspective on the patterns underlying the events . . . . Without this perspective they may find time and again they have addressed symptoms rather than causes, or have incorrectly evaluated the *personal* successes or failures of events whose outcomes have had deep roots in the intersection of the economic, technological, social and human dimensions of the organizational setting in which they work . . . . Thus, there is a role for concepts in ordering and giving coherent meaning to the phenomena a practitioner encounters as he goes about his work.[2]

Utilizing a behavioral-systems approach as the basis of conceptualization has great merit in integrating the rehabilitation and managerial processes. We believe that this will become evident to the reader as he moves through this text.

2. *This text is designed so that the practitioner can get as broad a perspective on new approaches to the management of rehabilitation workshops as possible, while limiting its size and scope so as not to become unnecessarily redundant or overly lengthy.*

In so doing, we have tried to consider only those broad areas that we feel will be of the greatest interest and of the greatest importance to the effective management of rehabilitation workshops. We believe that this approach will prove fruitful to those whose time is limited, and to those who want to spend their time in the most productive manner.

3. *This text is designed to encourage the reader to seek and research additional references which have direct application towards incorporating workshop management under a behavioral-systems approach.*

---

[2]G. F. Lombard, "Forward" in J. A. Seiler, *Systems Analysis in Organizational Behavior* (Homewood, Irwin Dorsey Inc. and the Dorsey Press, 1967), p. vii.

We do not suggest that this text, of and by itself, is an adequate source for the multitude of problems faced by the administrators and administrative staffs in the workshop context. Rather, we intend this text to be a source from which the practitioner can draw upon other references for a particular application or a better conceptual understanding. In order to accommodate this objective, we have provided practitioners with annotated notes which provide additional insight and more specific information into materials cited in the text. We hope that these additional references will stimulate the practitioner to inquire further into the complex and myriad variables which constitute human behavior.

In order to set the stage for the behavioral-systems approach taken in this text, we will first look at the traditional or classical schools of management theory. This should prove useful as a point of departure from which the reader can gain insight into a process by which he can compare other approaches which follow.

From this point we develop and consider at length the contributions made by the human relations theorists. Special emphasis is placed on the role of the workshop practitioner in dealing with the closely related problems of employee motivation and leadership. Succeeding sections of the text devote themselves to questions of structure, function, and technique.

Finally, no text in managerial practice would be complete without a review of the environmental constraints facing the workshop manager of the future. We have previously indicated that the future and the present may well be one and the same!

We close where we began, in suggesting that a behavioral-systems approach is quite probably the most efficient way of integrating the individual's goals with the larger objectives of the organization. How effective we have been in this task, we leave to our readers.

Douglas B. Simpson
Philip M. Podsakoff

ACKNOWLEDGMENTS

WHILE IT IS DIFFICULT to single out the numerous colleagues, teachers, and students who either directly or indirectly contributed to this book, we are especially indebted to a number of faculty members at California State University, Fresno.

To Dean Irwin Weinstock of the School of Business, we wish to express our special thanks for his assistance and encouragement toward making this book become a reality. To Joseph Townsend, Coordinator of the Master's Program in Rehabilitation Counseling, our sincere appreciation for the generous use of both his time and materials. And finally to Professor Ray D. Loyd of the Industrial Arts and Technology Department, our gratitude for the careful development and final design of the illustrative materials which appear in the text.

No work of this nature could emerge without the genuine interest of the individual who typed and proofread the manuscript and generally aided in its preparation for publication. For her special role, we express our deep appreciation to Mrs. Jan Arrants of the Department of Management and Marketing.

We are also indebted to Dr. John W. Payne, Executive Director of Goodwill Industries, San Joaquin Valley, Inc., whose insight into the management problems faced by rehabilitation practitioners provided material for many of the topics presented in this text. Likewise, Joe Klier, Assistant Chief of Field Support Services, California State Department of Rehabilitation, provided us with stimulating and provocative questions which inspired us to operationalize many of his ideas into the subject matter.

Finally, we wish to thank those who have most inspired our efforts—the handicapped. If this text helps to improve their situation, it will have been well worth it.

As always, we readily absolve all of the above for the failings of this book, but are equally intent on recognizing the very special contributions which inspired us to finish it.

Douglas B. Simpson
Philip M. Podsakoff

CONTENTS

WORKSHOP MANAGEMENT

Chapter 1

MANAGERIAL PRINCIPLES

INTRODUCTION

MANAGEMENT PRACTICES IN DEALING with human problems know no boundaries. In recent years, separate schools of "administration" have replaced the notion that the exclusive province of managing people is to be found in the country's business schools. In short, managerial principles are applicable in *any* organizational context, whether it be a corporation in the private sector or a sheltered workshop in the public domain.

We would not deny that there are special problems and unique circumstances which typify a workshop arrangement, but at the same time we feel the need to point out that there are also a number of similarities which are present. Throughout this book, we will proceed on this assumption, being careful to avoid generalizations which are not appropriate to the workshop setting.

EARLY MANAGERIAL THOUGHT

A systematic body of knowledge covering managerial principles is a product of the late nineteenth and of the twentieth centuries. Distilled from early capitalists such as Carnegie and Rockefeller, managerial principles were highly individualistic and rested more upon the unique personality of the industrialist than upon any well-defined body of knowledge. Jenks suggests "the state of the art" is:

> Problems of organization and the use of the labor force were solved *ad hoc*, empirically for each establishment. Knowledge about the solutions was transmitted by observation or word of mouth and had to be

3

rediscovered by most new firms. This type of thinking . . . predomi-
nated in American and British business concerns at the beginning of
the twentieth century. Here management was an uncertain mixture of
the traditional with the arbitrary or capricious—a personal autocracy
of varying degrees of benevolence—an emanation of the personality of
the owner-manager.[1]

It is generally believed that until the advent of the scientific
management movement and Max Weber's writings on
bureaucracy, little had been accomplished to coalesce the various components related to the management of complex organizations. The following sections discuss these developments.

SCIENTIFIC MANAGEMENT

The scientific management movement was given its initial
thrust under the direction of Frederick W. Taylor (1856-1915).
Taylor's ideas were strongly dominated by the Protestant ethic
of the time. Reliance on hard work, individualism, and the
related concept of economic rationality were the cornerstones
of this ethic.*

Taylor was a pragmatician who believed that by carefully
analyzing each task in an organization (primarily through time
and motion studies) one could arrive at the "one best way" for
performing each task. A related assumption was that workers
would be continuously motivated by the greater economic rewards resulting from the increased productivity in their jobs.
Further, Taylor's approach to management has been described
as an engineering or mechanistic orientation where the worker
was viewed as an adjunct to the machine. Increased worker
efficiency was the sole *raison d'être* of management.

Needless to say, this cold, calculating view of man's role in the

[1] L. H. Jenks, "Early Phases in the Management Movement," *Administrative Science Quarterly*, (December, 1960), p. 424.

*For a careful review of Taylor's contributions, see Frederick Winslow Taylor, "The Principles of Scientific Management," *Scientific Management*, (New York, Harper & Row Publishers Incorporated, 1947). It is interesting to note that current attempts at work simplification and measurement in workshop settings rely heavily on these early teachings.

productive process was not without its critics. Workers resisted time study techniques which attempted to standardize virtually every aspect of their performance. Managers also resisted Taylor's approach because of his reliance on the scientific method over their own judgment and discretion. In effect, many employers viewed scientific management as an unwarranted interference with managerial prerogatives.

ADMINISTRATIVE MANAGEMENT THEORY

In contrast to scientific management's attempts to optimize effort at the shop or operative level, a quite different body of knowledge emerged during the first half of the twentieth century whose primary emphasis was on developing broad principles which could be used to describe formal organization structure and the basic processes found in *all* management situations. This body of knowledge is frequently referred to as the traditional or classical theory of management, and can be stated in terms of five primary components: planning, organization, command, coordination, and control. These components in turn became the foundation for understanding basic processes or functions of management.†

Another contributor to traditional management theory was Mary Parker Follett. She is generally regarded as one of the first to view the organization in a behavioral sense. Her emphasis on management as a social process and the organization as a social system did much to free writers from an almost organizational myopia in neglecting the importance of the group process.‡

---

† Henri Fayol, an early French industrialist, was one of the leaders in advancing this general theory of management and has been described as the father of management theory. See Fayol, H., *General and Industrial Management,* trans. by Constance Storrs (London, Sir Isaac Pitman & Sons, Ltd., 1949).

‡ The necessity of viewing the workshop as a social system should be obvious to the reader. Perhaps in no other organization is the concept of informal group process as important. We will return to this notion in Chapter 5. See *Dynamic Administration: The Collected Papers of Mary Parker Follett,* H. C. Metcalf and L. Urwick, eds. (New York, Harper & Row, Publishers Incorporated, 1941).

Finally, two American writers must be considered in our review of early administrative management thought. James D. Mooney and Alan C. Reiley combined their business experience with a historical evaluation of the Roman Catholic Church, military organizations, and governmental agencies. Their analysis crystallized into four major principles: (1) a coordination principle, which suggested the need for unity of action in pursuing a common objective; (2) a functional principle, which organized work along departmental lines; (3) a staff principle, which carefully delineated the role of line management as exercising authority and the role of staff management as advisory and informational; and (4) a scalar principle, which advanced the notion of a pyramidal or hierarchial organizational structure. Modern day organization charts, job descriptions, and job specifications are a carry-over from these principles.§

BUREAUCRATIC THEORY

Mention was made earlier in this chapter of Max Weber and the bureaucratic model. Weber is considered one of the most important contributors to sociological theory, and it has only been until recent years that this brilliant social scientist has received the recognition he deserves. It is fair to say that his writings reflect not only administrative concepts, but also the much broader notions of economic and political structure. In short, Weber's views concerning bureaucratic organization were only a part of a total social theory.

Unlike the popular view of bureaucracy with its charges of red tape and rigidity, Weber believed that the bureaucratic model could be the most efficient structure devised, *provided* the following features were observed.

---

§ Heavy emphasis on the role of the church (both past and present) in the development of workshops suggest that these early studies can undoubtedly play an important part in explaining how workshops were formed. See N. Nelson, *Workshops for the Handicapped in the United States,* (Springfield, Charles C Thomas, Publisher, 1971). For further discussion of Mooney and Reiley's "principles," see J. D. Mooney and A. C. Reiley, *Onward Industry* (New York, Harper & Row, Publishers Incorporated, 1931).

1. "A continuous organization of official functions bound by rules." Rules save effort by obviating the need for deriving a new solution for every problem and case; they facilitate standardization and equality in the treatment of many cases.
2. "A specific sphere of competence. This involves (a) a sphere of obligations to perform functions which have been marked off as part of a systematic division of labor; (b) the provision of the incumbent with the necessary authority to carry out these functions; and (c) that the necessary means of compulsion are clearly defined and their use is subject to definite conditions." Thus a systematic division of labor, rights and power is essential for rational organization.
3. "The organization of offices follows the principle of hierarchy; that is each lower office is under the control and supervision of a higher one."
4. "The rules which regulate the conduct of an office may be technical rules or norms. In both cases, if their application is to be fully rational, specialized training is necessary. It is thus normally true that only a person who has demonstrated an adequate technical training is qualified to be a member of the administrative staff . . . ." This is tantamount to saying that the root of authority of the bureaucrat is his knowledge and his training.
5. "It is a matter of principle that the members of the administrative staff should be completely separated from ownership of the means of production or administration . . . . There exists, furthermore, in principle, complete separation of the property belonging to the organization, which is controlled within the spheres of the office, and the personal property of the official . . . ." This segregation presumably would keep the official's bureaucratic status from being infringed by the demands of his nonorganizational status.
6. "A complete absence of appropriation of his official positions by the incumbent is required." Rather than having organizational positions monopolized by an incumbent

they have to be free to be allocated according to the needs of the organization.

7. "Administrative acts, decisions, and rules are formulated and recorded in writing . . . ." Most students of bureaucracy see this requirement as less essential or basic to rational organization than the preceding ones. In more modern parlance, this act would be seen as contributing to "red tape."

Weber implies that any deviation from this "ideal" bureaucratic framework reduces the efficiency with which the organization operates.**

CRITIQUE OF TRADITIONAL VIEWS

One of the major criticisms of classical or traditional theories (scientific management, administrative management theory, bureaucratic theory) is that they employed closed-system assumptions about organizations which were unrealistic. As James D. Thompson states it:

> It seems clear the rational-model approach uses a closed-system strategy. It also seems clear that . . . developers of the . . . schools using the rational model have been primarily students of performance or efficiency, and only incidentally students of organizations. Having focused on control . . . as a target, each employs a closed-system of logic and conceptually closes the organization to coincide with that type of logic . . . .[1]

Still another criticism of the traditional view concerns its unrealistic assumptions about human behavior. Most of the so-called "principles" may be little more than truisms or com-

**See Max Weber, "The Essentials of Bureaucratic Organization: An Ideal-Type Construction," in Merton, R. K., et al., ed. *A Reader in Bureaucracy* (Glencoe, The Free Press, 1952). It is again interesting to point out the importance of religious doctrines in explaining organizational phenomena. Weber suggested that Protestants tend to emphasize the technical, industrial, and commercial, whereas Catholics prefer the humanities. Clearly, Weber submits, there is a basic value difference between people in these two religious groupings. This difference is the "spirit of capitalism."

[1] J. D. Thompson, *Organizations in Action* (New York, McGraw-Hill Book Company, 1967), p. 6.

mon sense, lacking guidelines for application. More important-
ly, these "principles" were based almost exclusively on personal
experience and anecdotal evidence and have not undergone
empirical measurement using scientific methods.

By far the most important area of criticism, however, concerns assumptions about the role of man in the organization.
Bennis submits that the central focus of the traditionalists or
classicists is to describe "organizations without people."[2] The
machine model, predicated on efficiency and rationality,
viewed man as simply another input into the productive process, and largely ignored the human variable.

In Chapter 2 we will discuss some of the major shifts that
have taken place in management thinking from the more traditional views. It is necessary to point out, however, that the
foregoing classical concepts still occupy an extremely important
place in management thought. It is fair to say that without the
contributions of Taylor, Follett, Weber, and others, we would
not have been in a position to understand many of the more
complex organizational questions which have arisen since these
early writings. In short, traditional management theory provides us with an important link to the past. Historical thought
in management, just as in other disciplines, is frequently useful
in prediction of the future.

---

[2] W. G. Bennis, "Leadership Theory and Administrative Behavior," *Administrative Science Quarterly*, (December, 1959), pp. 259-301.

Chapter 2

HUMAN RELATIONS AND

BEHAVIORAL APPROACHES

THE EARLY HUMAN RELATIONISTS

A S INDICATED IN THE PRECEDING chapter, many people were dissatisfied with the rigidities that they met in the traditional or classical schools of management. The failure of these early theorists to consider the human factor left many observers of managerial practice with an uneasy feeling that something had been left out. A series of research studies conducted at the Hawthorne Plant of the Western Electric Company between 1927 and 1932 was to change all this. The research began as a straightforward attempt at determining relationships between work environment and productivity. The results of the experiments conducted led the researchers to conclude that they were dealing with classes of psychological and sociological phenomena which could not be adequately explained with the tools of analysis developed up to this time. For the first time, the organization was shown to be more than merely a formal arrangement of functions. Rather it was a system of cliques, rituals, grapevines, and informal status systems. The Hawthorne experiments further demonstrated that people in the organization wanted to participate and to be recognized, as opposed to earlier assumptions that people were passive instruments interested only in fulfilling their economic needs.*

---

*A complete discussion of the Hawthorne studies may be found in F. J. Roethlisberger and W. J. Dickson, *Management and the Worker,* 11th printing (Cambridge, Harvard University Press, 1956).

THE HAWTHORNE STUDIES

The Hawthorne studies provided a much needed alternative explanation of human behavior in a work setting. It gave management, through the human relations movement, a new set of assumptions and criteria for understanding human behavior in an organizational setting.

Because of the importance of these studies in the development of the human relations movement, we will identify the phenomena which were researched. The initial study, which was to be followed by a series of other investigations, attempted to assess the relationship between the intensity of illumination and the efficiency of workers as measured by output. The experimenters felt that a positive correlation between increased room lighting and employee's productivity should exist. Despite the use of good research methods (such as careful selection of control groups) the experiment failed to confirm the sought for relationship between intensity of light and productivity. In fact, when the experiment was reversed (reduced lighting in the experimental setting) productivity *increased* rather than declined as predicted. Clearly, other variables were at work which were affecting output. The next five years were spent in an attempt to identify just what these variables might be. Successive studies dealt with the length of the working day, frequency and timing of rest periods, and a host of other factors relating to working conditions in the plant. Once more, it was found that regardless of changes introduced, production continued to increase. The researchers concluded that increased production levels bore directly on prevailing social conditions, employee motivation, and differing leadership patterns of supervisors, and had little to do with the physical surroundings.†

---

† The truth of this statement should be obvious to most workshop managers. Highly motivated and productive employees, in what must be described as deplorable working conditions, continue to make many workshops profitable and efficient. We are not suggesting, however, that workshops should continue in this manner, but rather that the physical environment be placed in its proper perspective along with more crucial factors such as the psychological well-being of the employee.

A later stage of the Hawthorne studies relied on nondirective, in-depth interviews of some 21,000 people. It is helpful to extract some generalizations from these interviews.

1. An employee's complaint is not necessarily an indication that the employee is malcontent, but rather the complaint may be a symptom of a personal disturbance which is deeply seated in the employee's subconscious level.
2. Objects, persons, and events have social significance to each individual. They may be positively or negatively related to employee satisfaction or dissatisfaction.
3. The personal situation of a worker is a network of relationships consisting of his sentiments, desires, and interests. The person's social past and his present relationships with the people with whom he works constitute his sphere of social reference.
4. The position or status of a worker is an important reference point from which he assigns personal meaning and value to other features of his environment, such as hours of work, wages, etc.
5. The social demands of a worker are influenced by social relationships and experiences both inside and outside of the working environment.‡

Despite the fact that the human relations movement has made a considerable impact upon present-day managerial style and thought, it should be pointed out that there has been serious criticism leveled against this school's tenets and philosophies. In the first place, the human relationists placed far too much emphasis on the psychological and sociological aspects of the working place; often at the expense of the technical and structural features of the job. Secondly, little concern was shown for outside forces (such as unions or political parties) and the impact such groups were likely to have on the organization and its members. In effect, the human relationists' view was rather myopic, based largely on a closed-systems approach toward explaining organizational phenomena.

---

‡ This is a brief review of some of the major findings. For a more complete treatment, see D. C. Miller and W. H. Form, *Industrial Sociology* (New York, Harper & Row, Publishers Incorporated, 1951), p. 58.

CLIENT-CENTERED THERAPY, SOCIOMETRIC THEORY, AND GROUP DYNAMICS

Three other early behavioral scientists must be mentioned in connection with the human relationists movement. Carl Rogers§ expanded the use of nondirective interviewing and counseling techniques developed in the Hawthorne studies and elsewhere to include a neo-Freudian approach which he later labeled client-centered therapy. Essentially, this nondirective approach emphasizes permitting the interviewee (rather than the interviewer) to direct the interview, at least in the early stages. Further, considerable importance is placed on *feelings;* not just factual information given in the counseling sessions. The nondirective counseling session has three functions:

1. It can help to provide clues to what the employee (interviewee) is *really* thinking and what lies at the root of the problem.
2. It can help the employee to experience *catharsis* (from the Greek: to make pure) or at least provide a channel through which frustration and tension may be partly reduced.
3. It can help the employee to develop greater insight into his own problems. To the extent that solutions are reached in this fashion, they are much more likely to be implemented than are those suggested by a supervisor.

Unfortunately, like all interpersonal techniques, nondirective counseling has a number of serious drawbacks, including the following:

1. Although counseling might help an employee feel better, or make an adjustment to a poor working environment (possibly a bad relationship with a supervisor) it frequently cannot improve the environment itself. In short, an employee may end up almost as frustrated as before.
2. Nondirective counseling techniques are directed almost

---

§ C. R. Rogers, *Counseling and Psychotherapy* (Boston, Houghton Mifflin Company, 1942). For a more recent treatment of these techniques see C. R. Rogers, et. al., *Client-Centered Therapy: It's Current Practice, Implications and Theory* (Boston, Houghton Mifflin Company, 1951).

exclusively toward changing *individual* attitudes and behavior in spite of considerable evidence that *group* attitudes are more important.
3. Counseling often divides line and staff management. For
example, employees often bypass their supervisors or
compare the "good" counselor with the "bad" supervisor.

Another important contributor to the understanding of
human behavior in organizations was Jacob Moreno.[1] Moreno
pioneered the use of sociometric tests, sociograms, role playing,
and psychodrama. Sociometric tests determine the structure of
groups and the interaction between group members. The
technique involves asking each group member to list his pre-
ferred choices according to criteria such as friendship or task
accomplishment. The data resulting from the test is then presented graphically in a sociogram. Interpretation of the sociogram permits many insights into the nature of the group and its
myriad relationships. Group leaders (stars) and least-accepted
members (isolates) are easily identified from the sociogram. In
addition, it is possible to analyze patterns of communication,
group cohesiveness, formation of cliques, and status relationships through the use of sociometric techniques. Thus, in a
workshop setting a "typical" sociogram might resemble that in
Figure 1.

The workshop manager (supervisor) will recognize some obvious limitations of using sociometric techniques. In the first
place, the physical proximity of the various work stations may
indicate the kind and form of interactions transacted. Secondly,
if it is a large workshop, it will be virtually impossible to identify
all of the various permutations and combinations which may
exist. Third, the fact that the group is aware that it is being
observed may elicit artificial or socially acceptable behavioral
patterns which do not represent the true picture of the workshop setting. Finally, it may be extremely difficult to
operationalize the findings, e.g. transfer the isolate into
another work setting where he can become more functional.
Despite these shortcomings, assessing and evaluating the na-

---

[1]J. L. Moreno, *Who Shall Survive?* (Beacon, Beacon House Inc., 1953).

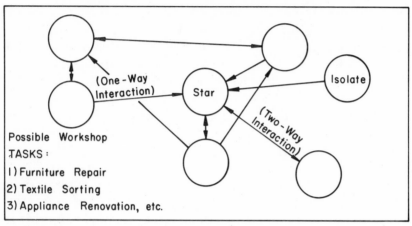

Figure 1. Sociogram of a Workshop Setting

ture and quality of workshop behavior would seem desirable if from no other standpoint than helping handicapped people to better adjust to different group processes. This is tantamount to saying that some group members will relate better to "selected" others rather than leaving their placement to chance.

No discussion of early contributions to management and behavioral science would be complete without a review of group dynamics and field theory. Unquestionably the seminal writer in this field was Kurt Lewin.[2] Lewin's approach to motivation theory was a major departure from earlier physiological explanations (stimulus—response). Essentially, Lewin theorized that a system in a state of tension exists within a person whenever a psychological need or an intention exists. Tension is presumably released when the need or intention is fulfilled. Key concepts associated with tension are *valence, force,* and *locomotion. Valences,* which may be either negative or positive, are psychological fields or regions for an individual at a fixed point in time. The construct *force* characterizes the direction and strength of the tendency to change at a given time. Change may occur either by a *locomotion* (a change in position)

---

[2] K. Lewin, *Field Theory in Social Science,* D. Cartwright, ed. (New York, Harper & Row, Publishers Incorporated, 1951).

of the person in his psychological environment, or by a change
in the structure of his perceived environment.

Lewin has also employed his structural concepts, in conjunc-
tion with his dynamic concepts, to give insight into the nature
of *conflict situations.* He distinguishes three fundamental types
of conflict.

1. An individual may stand midway between two positive
   valences of approximately equal strength. An illustration
   of this conflict situation might be where a handicapped
   worker is torn between satisfying a social need (such as
   being recognized and receiving approval from his peers)
   and satisfying an externally imposed societal need (such as
   conforming to the norm that all people *must* subscribe to
   the protestant work ethic). This situation could place the
   individual in an untenable position, in that in order to
   achieve his own *personal* goals he frequently runs the risk
   of alienating the group.

2. An individual may stand between two approximately
   equal negative valences. For instance, a handicapped
   worker may be aware that there are dangerous or
   nonhygienic work practices associated with his job; yet to
   discuss these practices with outside agencies may place
   him in the role of an informer.

3. The third type of conflict occurs when an individual is
   exposed to opposing forces derived from a positive *and* a
   negative valence. An example of this situation would be
   where a mildly handicapped person wishes to join a social
   group consisting of similarly handicapped people, yet is
   aware that becoming a member of the group may take on
   a negative valence from society at large.

All three of the foregoing conflict situations are best
explained through a concept developed by Lewin called
quasi-stable equilibrium; simply stated, *"quasi-stable equilibrium"* is
a system in which one set of needs is balanced off against
another.** Essentially, this concept revolves around introducing

---

**For a more thorough treatment of this important concept, see K. Lewin, "Frontiers
in Group Dynamics," Human Relations, Vol. 1, No. 1, (1947), pp. 5-42.

change into an existing organizational framework (such as a sheltered workshop). For example, a typical work situation employing handicapped workers may be producing at 60 percent of the efficiency that might be expected on the basis of purely technical considerations. Obviously, certain forces may be operating to hold the rate down. For instance:

1. Dislike of work
2. Fear of working oneself out of a job
3. An informally set "norm" (i.e. an agreed upon rate established by the work group)
4. Dislike of the supervisor

Yet another set of forces is probably operating to keep the rate *as high* as 60 percent. These may be:

1. Fear of losing one's job, or at least fear of losing special privileges
2. Pressure exerted by the supervisor
3. Financial incentives (both wages and fringe benefits
4. Fear of being caught idle

Presumably, at the 60 percent rate of production, these two sets of forces have reached a balance or *quasi-stable equilibrium* (See Point "A" in Fig. 2).

If management wants to increase production, the typical approach is to strengthen the upward forces (Point "B" in Fig. 2), perhaps by having the supervisor apply even more pressure or by indicating to the employee that others are producing more (greater fear of losing job). This method of introducing change is commonly referred to as *overcoming resistance.* The diagram predicts that the higher production climbs, the more workers' resistance is raised, until a new equilibrium is reached where the two sets of forces are once more in balance. However, at the *new* equilibrium, *stronger* forces are operating on each side, and tension is at a higher level. Frustration is greater, and employees are more likely to devise techniques to insulate themselves from the increased pressures and tension. From management's point of view this is an inefficient way of doing things. A more efficient way of accomplishing the same objective (i.e. increased productivity) would be to weaken the *downward* forces (Point "C" in Fig. 2), perhaps by making the work

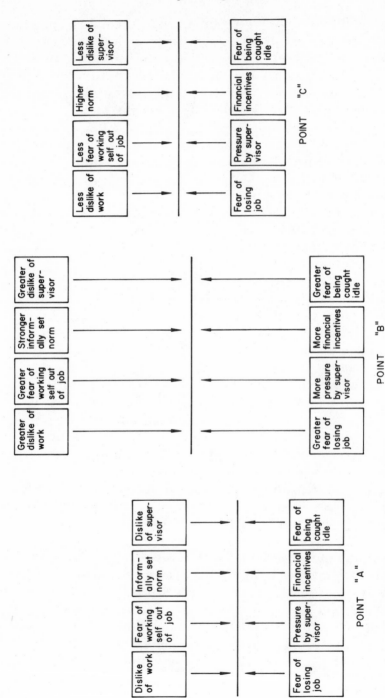

Figure 2. Lewin's "Quasi-Stable Equilibrium"

less disagreeable, or by reducing workers' dislike of their supervisor. This method is called *reducing resistance*. Here, too, a new equilibrium is reached at a higher level of production, but at a lower level of tension.

Thus far we have introduced some basic notions regarding the human relations movement, and early attempts to adopt behavioral science insights for organization theory and management practice. In Chapter 3 we will attempt to operationalize these and other behavioral elements toward an understanding of motivation. Probably no other area of management thought and practice has been so thoroughly researched. We further believe that the motivation of the handicapped employee, and subsequent attention to his needs and need satisfactions, is crucial toward providing an environment in which both the goals of the organization (productivity, efficiency, etc.) and the goals of the individual (recognition, esteem, status, etc.) may be met.

MOTIVATION AND INDIVIDUAL BE-

HAVIOR

O NE OF THE BASIC PROBLEMS in any society is how to motivate people to work. In our society this is not an easy task, since many people derive only slight personal satisfaction from their jobs, and enjoy little sense of accomplishment or creativity. The central question for all organizations would seem to be this: How can we create a situation in which employees can satisfy their individual needs while at the same time work toward the goals of the organization?* In order to provide at least a partial answer to this question, it is necessary to review some of the theories and concepts surrounding the motivational process.

MOTIVATION DEFINED

One possible definition for motivation is "an urge or tension to move in a given direction or to achieve a certain goal."† The presence of tension, energy, and drive in motion, is important in this definition. These variables combine in such a way that the motivational process is truly circular. Beginning with a tension or drive, an individual is acutely conscious of unfulfilled needs. In order to reduce this tension, a search process is

---

*While it cannot be denied that handicapped employees often have special needs which the organization (workshop) must consider, we will continue to suggest that these needs do not have to be incompatible with the larger goals of the workshop. Excessive attention to individual problems may obscure more serious issues which confront the workshop and its environment.

† This is a composite definition culled from various theories more commonly described as "drive theory." See J. W. Atkinson, *An Introduction to Motivation* (Princeton, Van Nostrand, 1964).

engaged toward fulfillment of these needs. Because it is highly unlikely that needs will be *completely* fulfilled, a refinement (or redefinition) of "new" needs takes place; where at least partial satisfaction is attained. This circular process is completed when the individual evaluates the extent of satisfaction obtained and begins to make decisions about appropriate behaviors which will lead to fulfillment of these needs (See Fig. 3.).

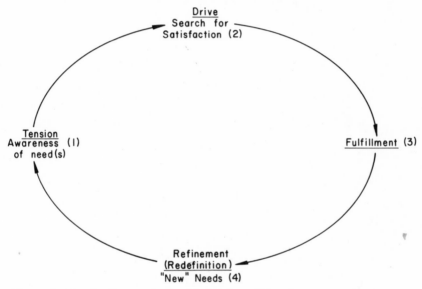

Figure 3. Circular Process in the Motivation of Employees

HIERARCHY OF NEEDS

Thus far we have argued that the behavior of an individual at a particular moment is usually determined by the existence of unfulfilled needs. It should seem important, therefore, for workshop managers to have some understanding about the needs which are commonly held by most people.

An interesting framework which helps explain the strength of certain needs was developed by Abraham Maslow.[1] Accord-

---

[1] A. H. Maslow, *Motivation and Personality* (New York, Harper and Brothers, 1954).

ing to Maslow, a five-step hierarchy of needs exists which can be classified into primary and secondary need priorities. Primary needs are the basic physiological needs required for the maintenance of bodily functions. They are primary because we attend to them first; other needs being satisfied after the basic needs are met. Secondary needs are psychological and sociological in nature and are strongly conditioned by culture, society, and our own personality or temperament (See Fig. 4).

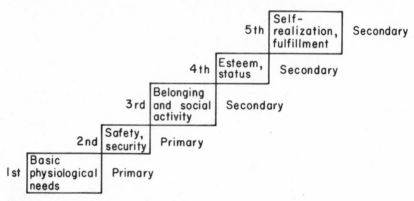

Figure 4. Order of Priority of Human Needs

The physiological needs include food, clothing, and shelter. The hierarchy predicts that until these basic (primary) needs are satisfied, the majority of a person's activity will be focussed at this level, with other levels providing little or no motivation.

The second step in the need hierarchy (safety and security) deals with the need to be free of the fear of physical danger and further deprivation of the basic physiological needs. In short, a need for self-preservation. A dilemma which presents itself, particularly in a workshop setting, is in determining just how far one should go in providing safety and security for an individual's development without weakening him. Stated in another way, too much safety and security may make an employee overly dependent and/or complacently unproductive.

Once physiological and security needs are reasonably well satisfied, the hierarchy suggests that belonging (acceptance) and social activity needs will become dominant. Since man is a social being, he has a strong need for affiliation with others. It is frequently argued that this need should be met mostly off the job. However, as approximately one third to one half of an employed person's waking hours are spent at work, developing meaningful relations with others in the work environment becomes crucial toward satisfying this need. We would further argue that the handicapped employee has special needs in this category, and that many workshop managers are not sensitive enough to the cues (both verbal and nonverbal) which indicates that this need is not being met.

After an individual has satisfied his need to belong, he usually wants to become *more* than just a member of his group. The need for esteem (both self-esteem and the esteem of others) takes on special importance. This esteem must be based on real capacity, achievement, and the respect of others. Further, satisfaction of this need is positively linked to feelings of self-confidence, prestige, status, power, and control. An indication that this need is not being satisfied often takes the form of apparent irrational or maladaptive behavior. Examples of such dysfunctional behavioral patterns would include work slow-downs or frequent arguments with co-workers or supervisors. Unfortunately, the usual response to such disruptions is a punitive one. Rather than perceiving the employee's frustration, and helping him to alleviate it, we too readily categorize the behavior as deviant and clamp further controls on his activities. This situation was discussed in Chapter 2 under the concept *quasi-stable equilibrium* (See Fig. 2, page 18). The net result is *increased* rigidity of behavior in which both the employee and the organization adopt the roles of protagonists.

Assuming, however, that esteem needs are at least partially satisfied, the self-realization needs become more prepotent, as shown in Figure 4. Self-realization is the need to maximize one's potential, whatever it might be. As Maslow stated it, "becoming everything that one is capable of becoming." Obviously, individuals can satisfy this need in different ways. In one handicapped employee it may be expressed in the desire to be totally self-sufficient; in another it may be expressed in training and directing other handicapped workers; in still another by receiving recognition from society-at-large for his demonstrated ability to overcome his handicap. (The Special Olympics for the mentally and physically retarded is an excellent example of the last possibility.)

In sum, individuals tend to satisfy their needs in order of priority. This is only an approximation, however, since the categories are not absolute. In reality, most people tend to be *partially* satisfied at each level and *partially* unsatisfied at the same time. The most important contribution, from management's point of view, is that once a need is relatively satisfied it no longer motivates the individual. This may be at least a partial explanation of why economic incentives go just so far in motivating an individual. Clearly, there are *other* needs present which may be equally potent in an individual's satisfaction repertoire.

THEORY X AND THEORY Y

A continuation of Maslow's work is seen in Douglas McGregor's dual concepts about the nature of man.[2] According to McGregor, there are two sets of assumptions about human nature and human motivation. Theory X assumptions state that most people prefer to be directed, wish to avoid responsibility, and want security above all. Theory Y assumptions hold that people can be self-directed and creative if properly motivated. Further, the properly motivated worker can satisfy his own needs best by directing his own efforts toward accomplishment of organizational goals. A more complete listing of McGregor's assumptions can be found in Table I.

Unquestionably, the real value of McGregor's work is not so much in choosing up sides as to which theory is "right," but rather to make our assumptions about human behavior more

[2] D. McGregor, *The Human Side of Enterprise* (New York, McGraw-Hill Book Co., 1960).

TABLE I
ASSUMPTIONS ABOUT THE NATURE OF MAN

Theory X

1. The average human being has an inherent dislike of work and will avoid it if he can.
2. Because of the human characteristic of dislike of work, most people must be coerced, controlled, directed, threatened with punishment, to get them to put forth adequate effort toward the achievement of organizational objectives.
3. The average human being prefers to be directed, wishes to avoid responsibility, has relatively little ambition, wants security above all.

Theory Y

1. The expenditure of physical and mental effort in work is as natural as play or rest.
2. External control and the threat of punishment are not the only means for bringing about effort toward organizational objectives. Man will exercise self-direction and self-control in the service of objectives to which he is committed.
3. Commitment to objectives is related to the rewards associated with their achievement.
4. The average human being learns, under proper conditions, not only to accept but to seek responsibility.
5. The capacity to exercise a relatively high degree of imagination, ingenuity, and creativity in the solution of organizational objectives is widely, not narrowly, distributed in the population.
6. Under the conditions of modern industrial life, the intellectual potentialities of the average human being are only partially utilized.

Adapted from D. McGregor, *The Human Side of Enterprise* (New York, McGraw-Hill Book Co., Inc., 1960), pp. 33-35; pp. 47-48.

explicit and to check how well our *own* behavior reflects our assumptions. Theory Y is clearly more dynamic; more optimistic about the possibility for human growth and development; and more concerned with self-direction and self-responsibility. Theory X implies that motivation will be primarily through fear and that the manager or supervisor will be required to keep close scrutiny over his subordinates if the organization's goals are to be met.

Adoption of either theory (and *both* have their supporters) directly influences how we organize for decision making and action. If we accept the premises of Theory X, then it would make sense to have:

—one-way communication.
—strategy planning by the top leaders only.
—decision making at the top level only.
—a handing down of decisions to be implemented by middle management.

—a handing down of instructions to be carried out by the workers (nothing to go up the hierarchy except reports). Theory Y would make it worthwhile to have:

—two-way communication.

—joint involvement in goal setting, planning, and decision making at each level.

—rejecting organizational controls in favor of self-controls.

As a final point, employees frequently experience the most frustration under a system which vacillates *between* the two theories. If the assumptions lead to inconsistent application, confusion and disorder is a likely result. It would probably be better that the practicing manager admit to *one* set of assumptions, and attempt to "live" within one framework.

MOTIVATION-HYGIENE THEORY

As implied earlier in the Maslow need hierarchy, esteem and self-realization needs tend to become particularly important when the more primary needs are realized. One of the more interesting pieces of research which deals with these two need areas was conducted by Frederick Herzberg.[3]

Herzberg set out to collect data on job attitudes from which assumptions about human behavior could be made. In a series of interviews, people were asked about what kinds of things on their job made them unhappy or dissatisfied and what things made them happy or satisfied.

After interpreting the data from these interviews, Herzberg concluded that an individual has two distinct and *separate* categories of needs which affect his behavior. He found, for example, that when people expressed dissatisfaction about their jobs, they tended to be concerned about the environment in which they were working. On the other hand, when people stated positive feelings of satisfaction about their jobs, the work (task) itself was the most important element. Herzberg labelled the first category of needs *hygiene factors* because they describe man's environment and serve to prevent job dissatisfaction.

---

[3] F. Herzberg, B. Mausner, and B. Snyderman, *Work and the Nature of Man* (New York, World Publishing Co., 1966).

The presence of these conditions, however, merely maintained a reasonable level of satisfaction in employees. Such conditions did not motivate employees to greater or more effective productivity. The second category of needs were called *motivational factors* since they appeared to be effective in motivating people to extraordinary or superior performance. A listing of both sets of factors, as perceived by Herzberg, are outlined in Table II.

TABLE II
MOTIVATIONAL AND MAINTENANCE FACTORS

Motivational	*Maintenance*
Work Itself	Status
Achievement	Interpersonal Relations
Possible Growth	Supervision
Responsibility	Working Conditions
Recognition	Job Security
	Policies and Administration
	Salary and Wages

Subsequent research in a wide variety of work situations has tended to confirm at least part of the motivation-maintenance model. The importance of Herzberg's research for workshop managers is to note that motivational factors such as achievement and responsibility are *directly related to the job itself*, the employee's performance on the job, and the recognition and growth which he receives from the task. Simply stated, the problem is that workshop managers, like their counterparts in other organizations, have often centered their attention on the maintenance factors, with predictably poor results. Fortunately, there has been increased understanding of why the maintenance (hygiene) factors have failed to motivate workers to be more efficient and productive. Once workshop managers and administrators better understand the difference between these two sets of factors, it is further hoped that they will place more emphasis on the latter factors because of their superior possibilities.

Before leaving the Herzberg model, it is necessary to deal with the most serious criticism directed at this research; namely, the identification of money (salary and wages) as a mainte-

nance or hygiene factor rather than a motivator. Unfortunately, relatively little is known about the psychological meaning of
money and how it motivates people. As discussed in Chapter 1,
pay or economic incentive was considered fundamental in the
scientific management approach to motivating the worker.
Later schools of management (Human Relations, Industrial
Humanism, etc.) in an attempt to establish the legitimacy of
social and self-realization needs, tended to overlook or
downgrade the importance of pay on the assumption that as an
individual accumulates more money, pay ceases to become important in the individual's need framework. This somewhat
puzzling interpretation of the value of money as a motivator
was quite possibly rooted in an inadequate understanding of
Maslow's need hierarchy. If one assumes that pay satisfies *only*
lower-level needs, then it is safe to say that once a person's
physical comforts are taken care of, pay will become unimpor-
tant as a motivator. If, however, pay is assumed to be linked to
satisfaction of higher-level needs (such as esteem, status, and
self-realization) then the "potency" of pay as a motivator is
clearly enhanced. While much of this argument may appear to
be purely academic to the workshop practitioner, it is important to realize that pay may well serve the same role for handicapped workers as it does for employees in general. In fact the
authors submit that pay increases which are a direct result of
recognized competency and achievement may well have a
stronger motivational pull for handicapped people than in
more "traditional" work situations. Research on this point in
workshop settings (both sheltered and nonsheltered) would
seem highly desirable.

   We have tried in this chapter to examine what is known today
about motivating employees. Various theoretical approaches
and treatments were discussed, which, in our opinion, indicate
that there are likely to be far more similarities and parallels
between the handicapped and non-handicapped worker than
dissimilarities. Having defined the motivational factors which
impact on the handicapped employee, we will now turn our
attention to another crucial behavioral characteristic—the role
of leadership in the workshop situation.

Chapter 4

LEADERSHIP AND THE WORKSHOP

EARLY ATTEMPTS INTO LEADERSHIP RESEARCH

F OR MANY YEARS THE most common approach to the study of leadership concentrated on leadership traits per se, suggesting that there were certain qualities, such as physical energy or friendliness, that were essential for effective leadership.* These inherent personal qualities, like intelligence, were felt to be transferable from one situation to another. Since all individuals did not have these qualities, only those who had them would be considered to be potential leaders. It was assumed then, that leadership behavior could be explained by isolating psychological and physical characteristics, or traits, which were presumed to differentiate the leader from other members of his group. As you can imagine, studies guided by this assumption generally proved none too fruitful, and the assumption itself has been subjected to increasing criticism. Two principle criticisms of trait research revolve around the validity of separating people into leader and non-leader "camps," and the nature of the traits themselves. The objection to traits is that the degree to which an individual exhibits leadership depends not only on *his* characteristics, but also on the characteristics of the situation in which he finds himself.†

---

*One of the earliest pieces of research into leadership "qualities" was reported on by Terman in 1904. Terman concluded that leaders who have a high average suggestibility are usually brighter, more noted for daring, more fluent of speech, better looking, greater readers, and more emotional than non-leaders. See L. M. Terman, "A Preliminary Study of the Psychology and Pedagogy of Leadership," *Journal of Genetic Psychology*, Vol. 11 (1904), pp. 413-451, as reported in C. A. Gibb, *Leadership* (Middlesex, Penguin Books, Ltd., 1969).

†The nature of the situation in a workshop setting is of course a paramount factor towards understanding the leadership process; probably more so than in most organizations.

It is perhaps not surprising that the traitist approach has proven rather sterile. Leaders do not function in isolation. They must deal with followers within a cultural, social, and physical context.

THE LEADER AND THE SITUATION

As implied earlier, more recent thrusts into the determinants of leadership behavior are essentially *situationist* in character. The situationists do not necessarily abandon the search for significant leader characteristics, but rather look for them in situations containing common elements. The case for the situational approach to leadership derives its strength from the fact that while organizations in general may exhibit broad similarities of structure and function, they also, in particular, show strong elements of uniqueness. More current literature seems to support this situational or leader behavior approach to the study of leadership.‡

LEADERSHIP BEHAVIOR DEFINED

Although there are many different definitions of leadership behavior, we have chosen to follow the definition provided by Fiedler, who in distinguishing between leadership *style* and leadership *behavior,* states: "By leadership behavior we mean the particular acts in which a leader engages in the course of directing and coordinating the work of his group members."[1]

Our rationale for selecting this particular definition over others is the inclusion of "acts," rather than placing emphasis on common or shared goals. The problem with the latter is that they are frequently highly abstract and/or not amenable to analysis and measurement. As indicated in both the preface

‡See J. K. Hemphill, *Situational Factors in Leadership,* Monograph No. 32, Bureau of Educational Research, (Columbus, The Ohio State University, 1959).

[1] F. E. Fiedler, *A Theory of Leadership Effectiveness* (New York, McGraw-Hill Book Co., 1967), p. 36.

and the introduction to this text, the dichotomies present in defining just what these goals should be, and how they might be reached, raises serious questions for workshop administrators.

LEADERSHIP BEHAVIOR IN WORKSHOPS

Unlike the problems of establishing and operationalizing goals, the task of indicating what leadership behaviors (acts) are likely to be important in workshops is somewhat easier. Two dimensions of leadership behavior have been developed by the Ohio State Leadership Study Group which have been tested over a wide and diversified number of sample populations.§

In studying leader behavior, the Ohio State staff found that two dimensions (*initiating structure*—"the leader clearly defines his own role and lets followers know what is expected;" and, *consideration*—"the leader regards the comfort, well-being, status, and contributions of followers") were separate and distinct. Thus, it was during these studies that leader behavior was first plotted on two separate axes, rather than a single continuum. Four quadrants were developed to show various combinations of initiating structure (task) and consideration (relationships) (See Fig. 5). From these and other observations, the Ohio State group conclude that a successful leader must contribute to both major group objectives: task accomplishment and group concern.

Another approach to describing leadership behavior is supplied by the group dynamics school. Cartwright and Zander, based on the findings of numerous studies at the Research Center for Group Dynamics, claim that all group objectives fall into one of two categories: (1) the achievement of some specific

---

§ For our purposes, inclusion of ministers, community relations leaders, and school superintendents, indicate that the findings should be reasonably appropriate to workshop managers. Many of the same functions (e.g. counseling, agency-client relations, training and development, etc.) are provided by all of the above groups. For a more complete description of the Ohio State Leadership material, see *Leader Behavior: Its Description and Measurement*, R. M. Stogdill and A. E. Coons, eds., Monograph No. 88, Bureau of Business Research (Columbus, The Ohio State University, 1957).

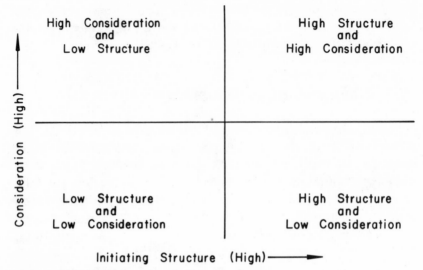

Figure 5. The Ohio State Leadership Quadrants
(Taken from Research Monograph No. 88, Bureau of Business Research [Ohio State University].)

goal, or (2) the maintenance or strengthening of the group itself.[2]

According to these authors the type of leadership behavior involved in goal achievement is illustrated by these examples: The leader "initiates action . . . keeps members' attention on the goal . . . clarifies the issue and develops a procedural plan."[3]

On the other hand, characteristic behaviors for group maintenance are: The leader "keeps interpersonal relations pleasant . . . arbitrates disputes . . . provides encouragement . . . gives the minority a chance to be heard . . . stimulates self-direction . . . and increases the interdependence among members."[4]

---

[2] D. Cartwright and A. Zander, *Group Dynamics: Research and Theory* (New York, Harper & Row Publishers, 1968), p. 496.

[3] *Ibid.*

[4] *Ibid.*

Referring back to Figure 5 we can say that goal achievement seems to coincide with initiating structure, while group maintenance parellels consideration.

THE MANAGERIAL GRID LEADERSHIP STYLES

A further extension of these concepts is found in Blake and Mouton's Managerial Grid.[5] In the Managerial Grid, five different types of leadership based on concern for production (task) and concern for people (relationships) are located in the four quadrants identified by the Ohio State studies as illustrated in Figure 6.

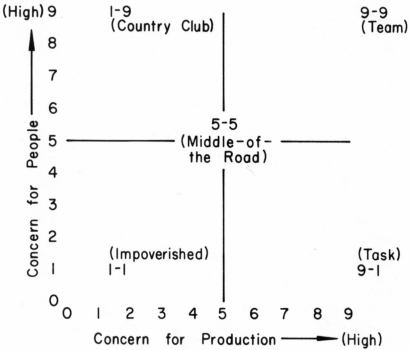

Figure 6. The Managerial Grid Leadership Styles
(Taken from R. Blake and J. Mouton, *The Managerial Grid* [Houston, Gulf Publishing, 1964].)

---

[5] R. Blake and J. Mouton, *The Managerial Grid* (Houston, Gulf Publishing, 1964).

Concern for production is illustrated on the horizontal axis. Production becomes important to the leader as his rating advances on the horizontal scale. A leader with a rating of 9 on the horizontal axis has a maximum concern for production.

Concern for people is indicated on the vertical axis. People (and interpersonal relations) become more important to the leader as his rating progresses up the vertical axis. A leader with a rating of 9 on the vertical axis has a maximum concern for people. The five leadership styles are described as follows:

Impoverished—Exertion of minimum effort to get required work done is appropriate to sustain organization membership.

Country Club—Thoughtful attention to needs of people for satisfying relationships leads to a comfortable, friendly, organization atmosphere and work tempo.

Task—Efficiency in operations results from arranging conditions of work in such a way that human elements interfere to a minimum degree.

Middle-of-the-Road—Adequate organization performance is possible through balancing the necessity to get out work while maintaining morale of people at a satisfactory level.

Team—Work accomplishment is from committed people; interdependence through a "common stake" in organization purpose leads to relationships of trust and respect.[6]

In essence, the Managerial Grid has given popular terminology to the five stages seen in the four quadrants of Figure 5.

In examining the dimensions of the Managerial Grid (concern for production and concern for people), one can see that these are *attitudinal* dimensions. On the other hand, the dimensions of the Ohio State model (Fig. 5) are *behavioral* dimensions (initiating structure and consideration). Thus, the Ohio State people direct their attention toward how people behave, while Blake and Mouton measure *predispositions* toward production and people.

While it is true that the two models discussed measure diffe-

[6] R. Blake, et.al., "Breakthrough in Organization Development," *Harvard Business Review* (November-December, 1964), p. 136.

rent aspects of leadership behavior, they are not necessarily incompatible. Conflicting views can arise, however, when behavioral assumptions are confused with attitudinal dimensions. For example, while high concern for both production and people would seem warranted in most organizations (including workshops), leaders exhibiting this dual concern for both people and production may not always find it appropriate to initiate both a high degree of structure *and* a high degree of socio-emotional support. In the context of a workshop situation where a leader's subordinates are mildly handicapped and can take responsibility for themselves, the "appropriate" style of leadership might well be low task and low relationships. In this case, the leader could permit maximum subordinate participation in the planning, organizing, and controlling of their own operation. In a situation where severely handicapped employees are involved, a 1-9 (Country Club) leadership style might be appropriate.

In summary, empirical studies tend to show that there is no normative (best) style of leadership; successful leaders frequently adapt their behavior to meet the needs of the group and of the particular situation.

A THEORY OF LEADERSHIP EFFECTIVENESS

Thus far we have discussed several approaches directed at understanding the leadership process. A logical extension of this analysis would be to consider the components which make up a given situation. Fiedler,[7] in what he calls a "Contingency Model of Leadership Effectiveness" has made one of the most significant advances in leadership theory by pulling together various behavioral elements into a coherent whole. Basically, Fiedler postulates that the effectiveness of a group is contingent upon the interaction between leadership style and the degree to which the group situation is favorable to the leader by providing him with influence over the group members.

---

[7] Fiedler, *A Theory of Leadership Effectiveness*, p. 247.

One of the major theoretical questions with which Fiedler's research deals is the prediction of leadership effectiveness. Leadership, in Fiedler's terms, is considered to be an interpersonal relationship in which power and influence are unevenly distributed so that one person is able to direct and control the actions and behaviors of others to a greater extent than they direct and control his. In such a relationship, the personality of the leader is likely to determine to a large extent the degree to which the leader can influence the behavior of his group. The theory postulates two major styles of leadership. The first style is primarily task-oriented, which satisfies the leader's need to gain satisfaction from performing the task. The other style is primarily oriented toward attaining a position of prominence and toward achieving good interpersonal relations. In terms of promoting group performance, Fiedler's research shows that the task-oriented type of leadership style is more effective in group situations which are either very favorable for the leader or which are very unfavorable to the leader. The relationship-oriented leadership style is more effective in situations which are intermediate in favorableness. *Favorableness* of the situation is defined as the degree to which the situation enables the leader to exert influence over his group.

The theory deals primarily with task (work) groups as opposed to social groups or other collectivities. Fiedler developed a classification system based on three major factors: *leader-member relations,* which indicates the degree to which the leader feels accepted by the group and relaxed and at ease in his role; *task structure,* which deals with the nature of the task (job) from completely structured (routine) to completely unstructured (permitting many exceptions, ambiguous, etc.); and *position power,* which describes the degree to which the position itself enables the leader to get his group members to comply with and accept his direction and leadership. When these three dimensions are combined in positive and negative relationships, they indicate the extent to which the situation is likely to be favorable or unfavorable to the leader.

Another definitional distinction is particularly important. By *leadership style,* Fiedler generally refers to the underlying need structure of the leader which motivates his behavior in various leadership situations. *Style* is measured by a sociometric instrument called Least-Preferred-Coworker (See Fig 7).

Think of the person with whom you can work least well. He may be someone you work with now, or he may be someone you knew in the past.

He does not have to be the person you like least well, but should be the person with whom you had the most difficulty in getting a job done. Describe this person as he appears to you.

	8	7	6	5	4	3	2	1	
Pleasant	8	7	6	5	4	3	2	1	Unpleasant
Friendly	8	7	6	5	4	3	2	1	Unfriendly
Rejecting	1	2	3	4	5	6	7	8	Accepting
Helpful	8	7	6	5	4	3	2	1	Frustrating
Unenthusiastic	1	2	3	4	5	6	7	8	Enthusiastic
Tense	1	2	3	4	5	6	7	8	Relaxed
Distant	1	2	3	4	5	6	7	8	Close
Cold	1	2	3	4	5	6	7	8	Warm
Cooperative	8	7	6	5	4	3	2	1	Uncooperative
Supportive	8	7	6	5	4	3	2	1	Hostile
Boring	1	2	3	4	5	6	7	8	Interesting
Quarrelsome	1	2	3	4	5	6	7	8	Harmonious
Self-Assured	8	7	6	5	4	3	2	1	Hesitant
Efficient	8	7	6	5	4	3	2	1	Inefficient
Gloomy	1	2	3	4	5	6	7	8	Cheerful
Open	8	7	6	5	4	3	2	1	Guarded

Figure 7. LPC (Least-Preferred-Coworker)
(Taken from Fielder, *A Theory of Leadership Effectiveness*, p. 41.)

The high LPC individual (who perceives his least-preferred-coworker in a relatively favorable manner) is visualized as a person who derives his major satisfaction from successful interpersonal relationships, while the low LPC person (who describes his LPC in very unfavorable terms) derives his major satisfaction from task performance. Correlations between leaders' LPC scores and group effectiveness indicate that the appropriateness of the leadership style for maximizing group performance is contingent upon the favorableness of the group-task situation. Group performance is related to both leadership style and the degree to which the situation provided the leader with the opportunity to exert influence. As indicated earlier, task-oriented (low LPC) leaders tend to perform best in situations which are either highly favorable or highly unfavorable. Considerate (high LPC) leaders tend to perform best in situations in which they had only moderate influence either because the task was relatively unstructured, or because they were not too well accepted even though their position power was high and the task structured.

In conclusion, leadership performance depends as much on the organization as it depends upon the leader's own attributes. It is simply not meaningful to speak of an effective leader or of an ineffective leader; we can only speak of a leader who tends to be effective in one situation and ineffective in another. If we wish to increase organizational and group effectiveness, we must learn not only how to train leaders to be more effective, but also how to build an organizational environment in which a leader can perform well. In the following chapter we will discuss ways of describing this environment, with a view towards providing a more complete definition of workshops.

Chapter 5

THE SYSTEMS APPROACH AND THE

WORKSHOP

EARLY SYSTEMS CONCEPTS

THE NOTION OF VIEWING COMPLEX organizations as systems is not new. In 1935 toward the close of the Hawthorne Studies (discussed in Ch. 2), a sociologist by the name of Lawrence J. Henderson suggested that: "The interdependence of the variables in a system is one of the widest inductions from experience that we possess; or we may alternatively regard it as the definition of a system."[1]

In short, systems and their parts are interchangeable, with all parts affecting all other parts. To place this rather abstract idea in context, let us consider a workshop. A workshop is a social system in which the various discrete functions and roles behave in a highly interdependent manner. Supporting government agencies, boards of directors, workshop administrators, handicapped workers, and the community, all interact within a systems framework.

Stated another way, the workshop is comprised of an external system (its environment) and an internal system (the workshop itself) which are mutually interdependent. There appear to be at least three elements in a social system: *activities,* which include the tasks which people perform; *interactions,* which occur between people performing these tasks; and *sentiments* which develop between people. All of these elements are closely interdependent.*

—————

[1] L. J. Henderson, *Pareto's General Sociology* (Cambridge, Harvard University Press, 1935), p. 86.

* The three elements of activities, interactions, and sentiments were first developed in a model by George Homans. See G. C. Homans, *The Human Group* (New York, Harcourt, Brace & World, Inc., 1950).

Finally, one of the most important early contributors to the notion of systems was Kenneth Boulding.[2] Boulding classified systems in the form of a hierarchy, which consisted of the following levels:

1. *A static structure*—a level of "frameworks"; such as the anatomy of a system.
2. *A simple, dynamic system*—a level of "clockworks"; where predetermined, necessary motions were involved.
3. *A cybernetic system*—a level of self-regulating, control mechanisms; analogous to a thermostat.
4. *An open-system*—a level of self-maintaining structure; analogous to a living cell.
5. *A genetic-societal system*—a level of cell societies; analogous to a plant.
6. *An animal system*—a level of mobility, teleological behavior, and self-awareness; typical of lower-order animals.
7. *A human system*—a level of symbolic interpretation and idea communication; typical of the more complex goal-directed behavior of human beings.
8. *A social system*—A level of human organizations; typified by meaning, value systems, historical records, and the complex gamut of human emotion.
9. *A transcendental system*—a level of ultimates and absolutes; exhibiting systematic structures but unknowable in essence.

It is difficult to capture the spirit of the contributions that these early theorists made, except to state that they injected a whole new way of thinking about the organization. In the nature of behavioral and systems approaches, much that followed was heavily dependent upon these early theorists.

OPEN AND CLOSED SYSTEMS

A further distinction between systems, is to characterize them as either closed or open. Closed-system thinking is perhaps best

---

[2] K. E. Boulding, "General Systems Theory: The Skeleton of Science," *Management Science*, (April, 1956), pp. 197-208.

explained through the use of static or mechanistic models. Traditional management theories (discussed in Ch. 1.) are usually considered as good examples of closed-systems philosophies for the following reasons:

1. The organization was conceived as being largely *self-contained* (hence, statements about the organization were directed almost entirely to the *internal* structure).
2. The organization had an inherent tendency to move toward a *static equilibrium and entropy*. (*Entropy* is a term which originated in thermodynamics and means the tendency for a system to move toward a chaotic or random state in which there is no further potential for energy.)
3. The organization was defined almost exclusively in terms of *rationality* (hence, the analogy of the machine, with all its parts in working order).

Open-systems theories, on the other hand, rely on viewing the organization as a series of inputs, throughputs, and outputs (See Fig. 8). While these three characteristics are the main "ingredients" of open-systems, they are by no means the only considerations. Katz and Kahn,[3] in their brilliant work on the social psychology of organizations, suggest nine characteristics which are common to all open-systems:

Figure 8. The Organization as an Open System

1. *Importation of energy (inputs):* Open-systems import some form of energy from the external environment.
2. *The throughput*: Open-systems transform the energy available to them.

---

[3] D. Katz and R. L. Kahn, *The Social Psychology of Organizations* (New York, John Wiley & Sons, 1966).

3. *The output*: Open-systems export some product (or service) into the environment.
4. *Systems as cycles of events*: The pattern of activities of the energy exchange has a cyclical character.
5. *Negative entropy*: To survive, open-systems must move to arrest the entropic process; they must acquire negative entropy. The open-system, by importing more energy from its environment than it expends, can store energy and can acquire negative entropy.
6. *Information input, negative feedback and a coding process*: Inputs are informative in character and furnish signals to the structure about the environment and about its own functioning in relation to the environment. Negative feedback enables the system to correct its deviations from course.
7. *A steady state and dynamic homeostasis*: The importation of energy to arrest entropy operates to maintain some constancy in energy exchange, so that open-systems which survive are characterized by a steady state. A steady state is not motionless or a true equilibrium. There is a continuous inflow of energy from the external environment and a continuous export of the products of the system, but the character of the system, the ratio of the energy exchanges and the relations between the parts, remains the same. Dynamic homeostasis (a biological analogy) involves the maintenance of constancies by establishing a constant environment and by reducing the variability and disturbing effects of outside forces. Thus, the organism (organization) does not simply restore the prior equilibrium. A new, more complex and more comprehensive equilibrium is established. The basic principle is the *preservation of the character of the system* (See Lewin's quasi-stable equilibrium in Ch. 2).
8. *Differentiation*: Open-systems move in the direction of differentiation and elaboration. Diffuse patterns are replaced by more specialized functions.
9. *Equifinality*: Open-systems are further characterized by the principle of equifinality. According to this principle, a

system can reach the same final state from differing initial conditions and by a variety of paths.†

THE WORKSHOP AS AN OPEN-SYSTEM

Thus far we have described some nine characteristics of an open-system, with a view toward providing a framework for understanding the various functions and processes which impact on the workshop. In later chapters we will more carefully identify structural and technological considerations which both inhibit and encourage the organization (workshop) to cope with its environment. What remains in this chapter is to operationalize these nine system characteristics in terms which are more easily recognizable for the workshop practitioner.

(1) *Importation of energy (inputs)*: The workshop receives various forms of assistance (financial, political, social, and philosophical) from interested bodies in the community. These inputs are sources of legitimacy for the workshop and are constantly changing in both their direction and impact. Mention was made earlier of "crisis" funding. To the extent that government agencies perceive that the workshop is a viable institution in which certain goals are being met they will most likely continue to support the organization (e.g. rehabilitation of clients and their successful placement in non-workshop settings; innovation in programs resulting in increased capacity to offer more and varied services to the community; and administrative excellence, usually indicated by favorable public reaction and ultimate workshop profitability). Inputs in terms of the human factor (i.e. workshop personnel, both voluntary and paid members) are likewise a function of the referring agencies' assessment of the workshop's ability to deal effectively with these placements.

(2) *The throughput*: The transformation stage in the work-

† D. Katz and R. L. Kahn, *The Social Psychology of Organizations* (New York, John Wiley & Sons, 1966), pp. 19-26. These descriptions of the nine characteristics are largely paraphrased and compressed into simpler explanations. Katz and Kahn's treatment uses extensive analogies which are not particularly important for our purposes.

shop is accomplished primarily through the various training phases established to help the individual adjust to a work-type situation. This takes the principal form of development of technical and social skills. Financial inputs (and similar sources of funding) undergo an exchange process into equipment purchases, inventories, and related costs of operating the workshop (overhead, etc.).

(3) *The output*: The end product of the workshop is usually measured in terms of successful rehabilitation (and resulting placement) of the client. Customer or consumer satisfaction with the workshop's goods and services, is of course, imperative to the workshop's long-run survival. (This is not to deny that many workshops may operate inefficiently and still receive community support, but we submit that the prospects for such a workshop are severely limited.)

(4) *Systems as cycles of events:* While the "patterns of activities" as described above, *are* typically cyclical, the workshop (unlike many organizations) faces some unique problems in maintaining this balance. In the first place, the workshop must frequently rely on sources of funding which are by no means automatic or assured (i.e. "crisis" funding). Shifts in political thinking at federal, state, and local levels can have a considerable effect upon the workshop's solvency, and leave it in a precarious financial position. Secondly, it is by no means clear that workshop administrators have agreed upon common goals and objectives for the workshop. This situation is largely a function of the "workshop duality" process described by Nelson, and discussed in our Introduction and Preface.

(5) *Negative entropy*: The workshop, much like any other organization, must acquire the means to arrest or slow down entropic processes. For the workshop, this is largely a question of convincing others of its legitimacy and its required support. New sources of funding, new client-agency-workshop relationships; and more accurate methods of "tapping" community support, will be necessary if the workshop is to reach its potential. For most workshops, the luxury of being able to fall back on surpluses or reserves is a highly unlikely situation. Increased competition from other organizations (both private and public)

will only intensify this entropic process, and will, we believe, lead ultimately to a reduction of workshops leaving only the more efficient.

(6) *Information inputs and negative feedback*: To the extent that the workshop is functioning in accord with the needs and demands being made upon it, information (signals) from the environment are for the most part positive. Unfortunately, positive feedback is often deceptive as it frequently does not reflect the true state of affairs affecting the organization. Of far more importance, however, is the fact that positive information (or feedback) is not acted upon, and is often mistakenly construed as a vote of confidence for maintaining the status quo. It is for these reasons that *negative* signals from the environment are far more likely to change the course or direction of the workshop in response to information which indicates that the workshop is dysfunctional or maladaptive. An example of this situation would be where long time private contributors cease or cut back on the amount of support they give to the workshop. Still another expression of negative feedback would be the withdrawal of government funding. In both instances, the workshop must respond and take what it believes to be corrective measures for alleviating the situation.

(7) *A steady state and dynamic homeostasis*: Fortunately, many on-going workshop programs do have the ability to sustain themselves for long periods of time, promoting organizational stability and continued support from the environment. This is tantamount to saying that successful workshops enjoy the position of being able to affect outcomes. It is interesting to note that success need only be *perceived* by other relevant reference groups, hence, the importance of public relations and promotional information about the workshop may be critical to steady achievement. We submit that many workshops have largely ignored this function.

(8) *Differentiation*: The extent to which the workshop is able to "elaborate" on itself, is closely linked to its ability to resolve the question of "workshop duality." In short, some workshops may be better advised to adopt a specialist role, while others should proceed as generalists. Unfortunately, organizations

which differentiate successfully must *initiate* new programs and roles for themselves. A much more common posture for the workshop has been to react to community needs and demands, rather than anticipating them.

(9) *Equifinality*: This final characteristic is largely a descriptive one. Workshops *can,* and do, reach the same final state from differing conditions and by a variety of paths. Possibly the best example of this is to parallel a church-dominated workshop with a secular or private institution. Both workshops may start from a different base (with slightly different philosophies and objectives) but may wish to reach the same final states of rehabilitation and profitability. In short, the *means* may vary but the *ends* remain the same.

SUMMARY

In this chapter we have attempted to consider the workshop as an open-system. We have argued that an open-systems construct is a valuable tool for describing the workshop milieu as well as providing a framework for prediction and decision making. In the following chapter, we will outline *specific* measures which may be taken to ensure that these characteristics are being met. In organizational behavior parlance, this area is defined as organization development (OD).

Chapter 6

ORGANIZATION DEVELOPMENT

AND THE WORKSHOP

THE NATURE OF ORGANIZATION DEVELOPMENT

ALTHOUGH A WORKING DEFINITION of the phrase *organization development* could refer to a broad range of strategies and programs for improving organizations, we prefer to adopt a more specific meaning and interpretation of the field.

Organization development, for the purposes of analysis in this and succeeding chapters will take on the following definition:

> . . . organization development is a long-range effort to improve an organization's problem-solving and renewal processes, particularly through a more effective and collaborative management of organization culture—with special emphasis on the culture of formal work teams—with the assistance of a change agent, or catalyst, and the use of the theory and technology of applied behavioral science, including action research.[1]

While it will be necessary to provide further definitions for the use of some of the behavioral terms mentioned in the above quotation, a historical review of organization development (hereafter referred to as OD) should prove useful to our reader.

HISTORY OF ORGANIZATION DEVELOPMENT (OD)

There is general agreement that OD began to emerge about 1957 as an attempt to apply some of the values and insights of

---

[1]W. French and C. H. Bell Jr., *Organization Development: Behavioral Science Interventions for Organization Improvement* (Englewood Cliffs, Prentice-Hall, Inc., 1973), p. 15.

applied behavioral science to organizations. The late Douglas McGregor (see Ch. 3—Motivation and Individual Behavior) is considered one of the earliest behavioral scientists to develop and implement an OD program. Other "pioneers" associated with these early efforts were Herbert Shepard and Robert Blake* who launched one of the first laboratory training (sensitivity training) sessions in private industry. This program was an important departure from more "traditional" undertakings, as these early human-relations groups began to view themselves as internal *consultants* rather than *researchers*. As these early behavioral scientists gained experience, they moved from a pure training group (T-group) mode to working with formal work (task) teams (superiors plus subordinates) on problems which the organization was experiencing. In addition, the consultants began to work on *intergroup* problems that had developed between groups or task units.

A final note on the history of OD concerns the emergence of survey research techniques at M.I.T. and later at the University of Michigan. Employee questionnaires and attitude surveys directed at assessing employee morale and obtaining important feedback were implemented. The value of these early attempts could be described as follows:

> The results of . . . experimental study lend support to the idea that an intensive, group discussion procedure for utilizing the results of an employee questionnaire survey can be an effective tool for introducing positive change . . . . It may be that the effectiveness of this method, in comparison to traditional training courses, is that it deals with the system of human relationships as a whole (superior and subordinate can change together) and it deals with each manager, supervisor, and employee in the context of his own job, his own problems, and his own work relationships.[2]

---

*For two interesting accounts of the genesis of OD, see H. A. Shepard, "An Action Research Approach to Organization Development," *Management Record*, Vol. 22 (June, 1960), pp. 26-30; and R. R. Blake et.al., "Breakthrough in Organization Development," Harvard Business Review, Vol. 42 (November-December, 1964), pp. 133-155.

[2] H. Baumgartel, "Using Employee Questionnaire Results for Improving Organizations: The Survey 'Feedback' Experiment," *Kansas Business Review*, Vol. 12 (December, 1959) pp. 2-6.

The importance of viewing the workshop as an open-system (social system) takes on new dimensions when the above statement is carefully considered.

THE BASIC CHARACTERISTICS OF OD

Thus far we have provided an operational definition and traced through some of the early "ingredients" of OD. But what are its characteristics, and what does it purport to do for the organization (workshop)?

First of all, OD is an educational strategy designed to bring about *planned* change. The presence of planning is an important feature. The reader will recall earlier criticisms voiced in this book that many workshops tend to react to change, rather than to initiate change. OD is a process (*not* a temporary program) which allows an organization to anticipate what changes will do to the various parts of the system.

A second characteristic of the OD process is that the changes sought for are coupled directly with the demand the organization is attempting to cope with. A workshop facing a "crisis" funding situation, for instance, has little difficulty in recognizing and assessing the demand component. Less likely, however, is the situation where the workshop is unsure of its purpose (the workshop duality).

A third characteristic is that OD emphasizes *experienced* behavior. Thus, reliance on data feedback, sensitivity training (training directed at increasing personal awareness and knowledge about self and interpersonal behavior and increased effectiveness in interpersonal relationships) and confrontation meetings (meetings which deal openly and honestly with personal feelings) are used to generate information upon which planning and decision making should proceed.

A fourth characteristic involves the use of a change agent (initially an *outside* [external] consultant who is likely to be more objective in clarifying the problems that the organization faces).

A fifth characteristic of the OD process implies a "collaborative" relationship between the change agent and members of the client system. This is frequently difficult to achieve, particularly when the organizational atmosphere is clouded with suspicion and distrust. Nevertheless, if changes are to be implemented, it is imperative that the change agent be given a "free hand" in both diagnosing problem areas and following up on his recommendations.

A sixth characteristic is that change agents share a social philosophy, a set of assumptions about the nature of man (see McGregor's Theory X and Theory Y in Ch. 3, page 25), and a set of values about the world in general. These shared assumptions and values lead to the shaping of specific strategies and responses to client systems.

Finally, a seventh characteristic is that change agents share a set of normative (prescriptive) goals based on the above social philosophy.† The most common goals included are:

1. to increase the level of personal trust and support among organizational members.
2. to increase the likelihood of *confronting* organizational problems (both within groups and between groups) rather than avoiding problems or "sweeping problems under the rug."
3. to create a climate where formal authority is based on expertise and knowledge.
4. to increase the openness of communications laterally, vertically, and diagonally.
5. to increase the level of motivation and satisfaction in the organization‡

While the above statement of goals would seem desirable for *any* organization, the problem remains of how to: (a) inculcate these goals in the minds of organizational members, and (b) establish a strategy whereby the goals become operationalized. To accomplish these ends, we turn to the action research process phase of organization development.

---

† Much of the succeeding analysis is built upon Warren G. Bennis' description of the OD process. See W. G. Bennis, Organization Development: Its Nature, Origins, and Prospects (Reading, Addison-Wesley, 1969).

‡ For a similar set of objectives, see "What is OD?" *NTL Institute: News and Reports from NTL Institute for Applied Behavioral Science,* Vol. 2, (June, 1968), pp. 1-2.

STRATEGY IN OD: AN ACTION RESEARCH MODEL

The action research process is usually considered in terms of a model. As previously indicated, the model involves extensive collaboration between the consultant and the client-group in the gathering of data, the discussion of data, and the planning stage. Figure 9 summarizes most of the essential phases of an action research model with the following features: data gathering, diagnosis, feedback to the client-group, discussion of data by the client-group, work by the client-group, action-planning, and action.

The sequence of events shown in the model are cyclical, with the focus on new or advanced problems as the client-group learns to work more effectively together. Many of the steps may be compressed or eliminated when they are not appropriate to the problem at hand. Possibly the easiest way of understanding the action research process is to pose the most common problem facing a workshop (the "workshop duality") and "walk" this problem through the various stages of the model. In addition, it is hoped that our reader will gain valuable insights into the nature of psychological and sociological theory.

THE ACTION RESEARCH MODEL AND THE WORKSHOP

Background of the Problem

The workshop accepts people into its program who are not acceptable in competitive (private or public) industry. The workshop must produce products or services which are acceptable to the community of which it is a part.

Perception of the Problem

How can the workshop meet the demands of the community and at the same time serve the needs of the handicapped?

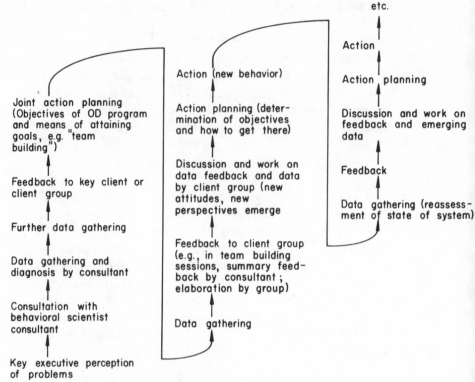

Figure 9. An Action Research Model for OD
(Taken from French and Bell, *Organization Development* [Englewood Cliffs, Prentice-Hall, 1973].)

Consultation

While Nelson has indicated that there are three possible ways of viewing the question posed (conflict, no conflict, and synthesis),[3] it is by no means clear that the individual workshop administrator understands the complex elements which make up a conflict situation. It is precisely at this stage in the process that the behavioral scientist consultant can, in our opinion,

---

[3] N. Nelson, *Workshops for the Handicapped in the United States: An Historical and Developmental Perspective* (Springfield, Charles C Thomas Publisher, 1971), pp. 190-194.

make a significant contribution. For example, the eminent behavioral scientist and sociologist, Caplow,[4] points out that all complex organizations are characterized by what he calls "mixed-motive-processes," in which are contained both conflict and mutual dependence elements among members and organizational subunits. Further, conflict is a function of four variables *which can be observed and measured.* These variables are: *subjugation,* which is the ability of one party to interfere with the program of another (and vice versa); *insulation,* which measures the extent to which communications are blocked; *violence,* which is a measure of the overt hostility that members in an organization develop toward each other; and *attrition,* which is the *cost* of conflict, measured by the price of the damage each party inflicts on each other.

Still another approach to the understanding of conflict is provided by Louis Pondy.[5] Beginning with identification of three models of conflict: *bargaining* conflict among parties to an interest-group relationship; *bureaucratic* conflict between parties to a superior-subordinate relationship; and *systems* conflict among parties to a lateral or working relationship. Pondy expands his treatment to include episodic stages of latency, feeling, perception, manifestation, and aftermath.[6]

Successive stages of conflict require more careful definition. *Latent* conflict can be condensed into three basic drives: competition for scarce resources, drives for autonomy, and divergency of goals. Put another way, when demands of participants for resources *exceed* the resources available, conflict results. The drive for autonomy produces conflict when one party either seeks to exercise control over some activity that the other regards as his own province or seeks to insulate himself from such control. Finally, goal divergence can result in conflict when two parties who must cooperate on some joint activity cannot reach consensus on concerted action.

Perceived conflict may exist when no conditions of latent

---

[4] T. Caplow, *Principles of Organization* (New York, Harcourt, Brace & World, 1964).
[5] L. R. Pondy, "Organizational Conflict: Concepts and Models," *Administrative Science Quarterly,* (September, 1967) pp. 296-320.
[6] *Ibid.,* p. 296.

conflict are apparent. In this instance, conflict can be said to result from the parties' misunderstanding of each others' true position.

An important distinction between *perceiving* conflict and *feeling* conflict is advanced by Pondy as follows:

> A may be aware that B and A are in serious disagreement over some policy, but it may not make A tense or anxious, and it may have no effect whatsoever on A's affection towards B.[7]

Manifest conflict is relatively rare in an organizational context, with slowdowns and less overt actions being more the norm. The most useful definition of manifest conflict seems to be behavior which *deliberately* frustrates the other party.

The last stage of conflict (*aftermath*) can lead to either resolution or some form of suppression (non-resolution).

We should point out that what might appear to our reader to be a rather abstract and highly conceptualized approach to conflict, is in reality the basis or rationale upon which the consultant/change agent can institute needed change or changes. This knowledge, coupled with objectivity, can better identify what *kind* of conflict is occurring and the location within the workshop *where* it is most likely to be a problem.

Diagnosis

Theoretically, the initial objectives of a program for OD spring from a careful observation of communication blockages, potential conflict situations, interpersonal and intergroup relationships, decision-making processes, and the like. At this stage, the behavioral scientist and the key client (the workshop administrator) make a joint, tentative assessment of the more critical problems facing the organization. This phase is frequently an interim step toward gathering more information, and should focus on the expressed needs of the client. Ironical-

---

[7] Pondy, "Organizational Conflict: Concepts and Models," *Administrative Science Quarterly*, p. 302.

ly, it is at this highly sensitive stage that the client may not be willing to release certain data which he perceives as reflecting on his managerial abilities or performance.§ The skilled consultant will anticipate this, and attempt to alleviate what is often nothing more than ill-defined suspicions and uneasiness.

FEEDBACK AND THE CONSULTANT'S ROLE

Frequently, it is advantageous to schedule several off-site sessions (similar to "retreat" activities) in team building or group problem solving to encourage openness among organizational members. Feedback and support is provided by the consultant, with a view toward letting individuals experiment with "new" behaviors. As participants experience increased confidence, they will typically move into more "high risk" activities, and it is at this juncture that problem resolution begins to take place. Throughout this process, the behavioral scientist usually adopts an observer's role, and intervenes only to the extent that the group expresses a need for such intervention.

It is necessary to point out that different workshop situations will experience different problems along a production-people continuum. (See Ch. 4. The Managerial Grid Leadership Styles, page 34.) Some workshops, for example, may be interested in clarifying *task* (production) objectives, while others may have the greatest need to strengthen interpersonal (people) relationships. In either instance, the consultant should play an important role in attempting to stimulate new behaviors which will be more productive and effective.

The remaining stages in the action research model are essentially of the monitoring type. That is to say, have the new behaviors resulted in positive *actions* directed at the problems? Follow-up should indicate whether or not habitual behavioral patterns are being "resurrected," or the new behavioral modes are being implemented.

---

§ For a more complete description of the diagnostic stage, see R. Beckhard, "An Organization Improvement Program in a Decentralized Organization," *Journal of Applied Behavioral Science,* Vol. 2 (January, February, March, 1966) pp. 3-4.

SENSITIVITY TRAINING AND T-GROUPS

While we have tended to indicate that OD has enormous potential for changing an organization, some of its methods (in particular, sensitivity training) have been subject to considerable criticism. In fact, a large number of organizations have abandoned sensitivity training entirely. Odiorne describes the major reason.

> [sensitivity training] creates a great psychological nudist camp in which he (the participant) bares his pale, sensitive soul to the hard-nosed autocratic ruffians in his T-Group and gets roundly clobbered. He goes away with his sense of inferiority indelibly reinforced.§§

The above type of situation can be emotionally devastating to some individuals because it penetrates those defense mechanisms that protect their sense of personal status and well-being. These remarks point up the importance not only of proceeding with caution in T-Group (sensitivity) training but also for following up with the participants when they return to their jobs. It seems almost unnecessary to point out that the above concerns were expressed about "normal" groups. The implications for the severely handicapped, would, of course, be much more intense and would require a carefully controlled psychotherapeutic orientation using rehabilitation counselors and other like specialists. The primary purpose of sensitivity training is:

> . . . to help men achieve a greater awareness of how human beings relate to one another . . . by bringing to the surface, for conscious examination, the normally unquestioned assumptions about human beings.[8]

We submit that this is every bit as important in the workshop setting as it is in the private or commercial sector. The fact that

---

§§As quoted by S. Know, "Inside a T-Group," *Think Magazine,* (1965).

[8] *Developing Managerial Competence: Changing Concepts—Emerging Practices,* Studies in Personnel Policy, No. 189 (New York, National Industrial Conference Board, 1964), p. 91.

the techniques and skills required may vary somewhat, does not negate the value of such a program.

In conclusion, we can say that successful OD tends to be (a) a total-systems effort; (b) a continual process of planned improvements, rather than a one shot or temporary program; and (c) a plan directed at developing the organization's most important resources, its people, for effective change in the future.

Throughout this chapter we have emphasized the importance of decision making. The following chapter will describe various approaches that the workshop practitioner might wish to consider.

Chapter 7

DECISION MAKING IN THE WORKSHOP

INTRODUCTORY CONCEPTS

DECISION MAKING IS ONE of the most important activities engaged in by individuals, groups, and organizations. Further, decision making is frequently considered as both a managerial function and an organizational process. It is managerial in that it is a primary responsibility of the manager himself. It is organizational in that most decisions go far beyond an individual manager and become the joint concern of client-groups, committees, and boards.

Regardless of the level at which decisions are made, the process appears to involve certain common elements. These would include: (a) *a search process* directed at finding a new goal or goals because of dissatisfaction with present outcomes; (b) *the formulation of objectives* after the search has been completed; (c) *the selection of alternatives* to accomplish the chosen objectives; and (d) *the evaluation of outcomes.**

It should become readily apparent to our reader that decision making is highly interdependent with the planning, leadership, and communication processes. In fact, it would be safe to say that successful implementation in these areas is contingent upon the care and attention shown in decision-making activities.

But effective decision making is something more than a synthesis of related activities; it is the product of a logical, systematic, course of action. Peter Drucker, a leading management thinker, refers to this process as a sequence of activities which he arranges into the following steps:

---

*Adapted from H. A. Simon, *The New Science of Management Decision* (New York, Harper & Row Publishers, 1960).

1. *The classification of the problem*—Is the problem exceptional and unique, or is the problem routine and "ordinary"?
2. *The definition of the problem*—What, precisely, are we dealing with?
3. *The specifications of the problem*—What are the "boundary conditions," i.e. the *limits* of the problems?
4. *The decision as to what is "right," rather than what is acceptable*—What will fully satisfy the specifications before attention is given to compromises, adaptations, and concessions needed to make the decision acceptable?
5. *The action(s) necessary to carry the decision out*—What does the action committment have to be? Who has to know about it, and who will carry it out?
6. *The feedback which tests the validity and effectiveness of the decision against what is actually happening*—How is the decision being carried out? Are the assumptions appropriate?†

These sequential steps are applicable throughout the decision-making process, and are considered as basic regardless of the organization which is being studied.

RATIONALITY IN DECISION MAKING

Decision making, as discussed in this chapter, is a human, mental process. In the lower phylogenetic orders of animal life, we frequently refer to decision-making behavior as being almost exclusively instinctual. The overt, behavioral acts which stem from instinct are almost completely automatic, and are directed, for the most part, toward survival of the species. In humans, however, the range of possible behavioral alternatives is infinitely more complex and far greater than those available, to other animals. This is so because of man's ability to learn and to pass on his knowledge to future generations in the form of written records and documents, long after he has ceased to

---

†Derived from P. J. Drucker, *The Effective Executive* (New York, Harper & Row Publishers, 1966).

exist. Man's behavioral repertoire is often considered analogous to a computer because of the human brain's ability to selectively store (and retrieve) a myriad of information "bits." These capacities make rational, problem-solving behavior possible. But rational decision making is considerably more than a synthesis of available alternatives (means). It is also a product of the respective ends to which the comparison of alternative means will lead. The dangers inherent in making a choice among these alternatives are very real, because:

> the ends to be attained by the choice of a particular behavioral alternative are often incompletely or incorrectly stated through failure to consider the alternative ends that could be reached by selection of another behavior.[1]

An example in the workshop would be the final selection between several contracts with outside firms. If we were to adopt Simon's view, it would not be sufficient to select a contract on the basis that it would satisfactorily meet desired goals. Rational decision making would require that *all* possible alternatives be considered in terms of the respective ends to which they would lead.

In summary, rationality implies that the decision maker attempts to maximize the values in a situation by choosing an optimal (best) course of behavior or achieving an optimal solution to a problem. Under conditions of "full" rationality (where the decision maker is aware of *all* the elements affecting the decision) it would be necessary to consider the full range of possible choices. Obviously, complete rationality in decision making is highly unrealistic. Not only does the decision maker face time limitations which impose constraints on the search process, but also must rely on imperfect or incorrect information upon which to make a decision. In addition, the organization often holds conflicting goals or objectives (the workshop duality). It is for these reasons that we must consider the "principle of bounded rationality."[2]

---

[1] H. A. Simon, *Administrative Behavior* (New York, The Macmillan Company, 1961), p. 65.

[2] Simon, *Administrative Behavior*, p. 52.

BOUNDED RATIONALITY

While Simon was an adamant spokesman for the rational decision-making process, he was also fully aware of the limitations which plagued the pursuit of rationality. To Simon, decision-making man was bounded by three major limitations:
1. the individual was limited by skills, habits, and reflexes of which he was not consciously aware.
2. the individual was limited by his values and conceptions of purpose which frequently influenced him in making a decision.
3. the individual was limited by the extent of his knowledge of things relevant to his job.‡

Theoretically, if a group of experts were given the *same* information (under conditions of rationality) they should reach identical conclusions. In reality, however, in light of the above perceptual limitation, there is more than a reasonable likelihood that they will not. In short, some factors are beyond an individual's control entirely, while still others are beyond the individual's capacity to learn of them.

Given these circumstances, a decision maker seldom tries to find the optimum (best) decision. Instead, he is much more likely to select a strategy which results in a satisfactory (satisficing) outcome.§

Finally, it should be pointed out that while decision making cannot be perfectly or objectively rational, this does not invalidate or negate the concept of rationality. Short of arriving at the "best" solution, a decision maker should recognize both his own and the organization's limitations and strive to raise the quality of his decisions to the highest level possible within these constraints.

---

‡ Based on Simon's triangle of limitations. See Simon, *Administrative Behavior*, p. 40.

§ *Satisficing* is also a function of habitual decision making. Those decisions which worked in the past are adopted again. For an expansion of Simon's work, see D. W. Miller and M. K. Starr, *The Structure of Human Decisions* (Englewood Cliffs, Prentice-Hall, Inc., 1967).

HEURISTIC DECISION MAKING

Along with the processes of rationality and bounded rationality, is a third approach to decision making which is usually described as heuristics (a sophisticated trial-and-error approach). Heuristics are frequently "rules of thumb" and rely heavily on past experiences and intuition. Heuristics are especially appropriate to the workshop manager in that they legitimize a process often referred to as "gut level decisions." Obviously, our heuristics may be good or bad, depending upon the relevance of our experiences to the problem at hand. Gore describes the heuristic process as:

> a groping toward agreements seldom arrived at through logic. The very essence of the heuristic process is that the factors validating a decision are internal to the personality of the individual instead of external to it.[3]

The heuristic model tends to formalize subjective decision making by taking into consideration the human element. More rational approaches assume cause-and-effect relationships which often ignore or play down the value of the human input.

Our resolution of this seeming paradox is to consider heuristic applications as an adjunct to rational decision making. It would be unfortunate, and in our opinion unnecessary, not to factor in the collected wisdom of workshop personnel. Human values and sensitivities while not amenable to quantitative analysis or precise (statistical) measurement, are frequently at the core of many decisions that we make about people. Attempts to "assume away" the behavioral part of the decision-making "equation" is to ignore a very rich or fertile source of information. In short, what a man *is* becomes a force that conditions the decisions he makes.

---

[3] W. J. Gore, *Administrative Decision-Making: A Heuristic Model* (New York, John Wiley & Sons, Inc. 1964), p. 12.

TYPES OF DECISIONS

It is frequently useful to distinguish between different types of decisions. In our opinion, decisions tend to fall into two general categories: (a) basic and routine, and (b) programmed and nonprogrammed.

Basic and Routine Decisions

Basic decisions are those decisions which are unique, one-shot decisions involving long-term commitments with a high degree of permanence for the organization.

An example of a basic decision in a workshop would be the selection of an appropriate site or business location. Questions of suitable markets, transportation availability for both the client group and the customers served, access to raw materials, etc., make the decision relatively permanent. Decisions on leasing arrangements for buildings are also of a basic nature, in that the workshop is "tied" to a decision for a stipulated period of time.

Decisions on organizational structure (see Ch. 9) should also be considered basic because of the dramatic effects they play in defining the interrelationships and activities in the workshop. In fact, most policy decisions are basic decisions because they establish the ground rules for other decisions and are likely to be relatively stable and far-reaching.

On the other hand, routine decisions are of a highly repetitive nature and require little deliberation by the parties involved. Routine decisions tend to make only a minor impact on the organization, and are frequently codified into procedures. For example, a handicapped worker who sorts and sizes clothing into bins makes literally hundreds of decisions of this type and does so according to an established procedure laid down by the workshop. Decisions of this kind can be easily modified or reversed.

As a final note on basic and routine decisions, it should be apparent to our reader that many decisions are mixed, having

elements of *both* types. Thus, it is useful to think of decisions as
falling on a continuum with the two poles representing extreme
positions (i.e. completely unalterable versus completely flexible).

PROGRAMMED AND NONPROGRAMMED DECISIONS

Adopting the language of the computer, Simon has developed a classification of decisions as either programmed or
nonprogrammed.[4] This typology is roughly parallel to basic
and routine decisions in that programmed decisions tend to be
repetitive, and nonprogrammed decisions, novel, unstructured, and somewhat unique.

The primary advantage of the programmed and nonprogrammed theory of decision making is that it more clearly identifies methods of decision making which are likely to accompany each type of decision. In addition, this approach lends
itself to a comparison with the more recent techniques of quantitative analysis which are available to the decision maker. Table
3 describes the two types of decision making together with their
corresponding techniques.

Thus far, we have discussed the various elements which go
into making a decision. We have deliberately avoided discussion of the circumstances under which the decision is likely to
be more or less effective. There is, in our opinion, a good
reason for excluding qualitative considerations from this chapter. That is: the effectiveness (or efficiency) of a particular
decision is not so much a function of the *kind* of decision being
made (basic/routine, programmed/nonprogrammed) but
rather a function of the *quality of information* which went into
making the decision in the first place. In general, "good" decisions are a result of "good" information. How information is
received and processed within the organization (workshop) is
directly related to the existing communication structure. The
following chapter will discuss communication barriers (and

---

[4] Simon, *Administrative Behavior*, pp. 5-8.

techniques to avoid them) as a means toward improving the quality of information that the decision maker receives.

TABLE III
TRADITIONAL AND MODERN TECHNIQUES OF
DECISION MAKING

Types of Decisions	Decision-Making Techniques	
	Traditional	*Modern*
Programmed: Routine, repetitive decisions. Organization develops specific processes for handling decisions.	1. Habit 2. Clerical routine: Standard operating procedures. 3. Organization structure: Common expectations. A system of subgoals. Well-defined information channels.	1. Operations research: Mathematical analysis. Models Computer simulation. 2. Electronic Data Processing.
Nonprogrammed: One-shot, ill-structured, novel, policy decisions. Handled by general problem-solving processes.	1. Judgment, intuition, and creativity. 2. Rules of thumb. 3. Selection and training of executives	1. Heuristic problem-solving. 2. Training human decision makers. 3. Constructing heuristic computer programs.

Taken from H. A. Simon, *The New Science of Management Decision* (New York, Harper & Row, Publishers, 1960), p. 8.

COMMUNICATIONS IN THE WORKSHOP

COMMUNICATION DEFINED

IN THE PRECEDING CHAPTER in decision making, we pointed out the importance of understanding the vital role that communication plays in the decision-making process. The close interaction and interdependency of these two behavioral variables is perhaps best expressed by Pfiffner and Sherwood:

> If decision-making and communication processes are not identical, they are so interdependent they become inseparable in practice.[1]

Taken collectively the communication process covers virtually every act that man engages in. Man is constantly developing and transmitting his opinions and attitudes. As the aim of the process is to transfer information and ideas from one person to another, communication is a process of creating and exchanging meaning. In short, the process is circular, complex, and involves much more than just a verbal component.

Other attempts at defining communication have included the following:

> ... communication may be defined as the field of inquiry concerned with the systematic use of symbols to achieve common or shared information about an object or event.[2]

> ... the transmission and reception of ideas, feelings, and attitudes— verbally and/or nonverbally—which produce a response.[3]

---

[1] J. M. Pfiffner and F. P. Sherwood, *Administrative Organization* (Englewood Cliffs, Prentice-Hall, Inc., 1970), p. 308.

[2] J. Kelly, *Organizational Behavior* (Homewood, Richard D. Irwin, Inc. and The Dorsey Press, 1969), p. 450.

[3] N. B. Sigband, *Communication for Management* (Glenview, Scott, Foresman and Company, 1969), p. 10.

Unfortunately, there is as yet no firmly established theory of communication which can provide us with set principles that will ensure effective communication. For our purposes, communication can be defined as the chain of understanding that links together members of an organization vertically, diagonally, and horizontally. The usefulness of this definition is that it allows us to place communication in an organizational context, as well as considering communication as an interpersonal (face-to-face) process. Regardless of the unit of analysis (individual versus organizational), the primary problem in communication is that the meaning which is actually received is not the meaning which was intended. What are the causes of breakdowns in communications? What can be done to overcome them? We shall consider each of these questions in turn.

BARRIERS TO EFFECTIVE COMMUNICATION

INDIVIDUAL DIFFERENCES IN EXPERIENCES AND "FRAMES OF REFERENCE": What we hear or understand is largely shaped by our own experience and background. Most people have preconceived ideas of what people mean and will go to considerable lengths to adjust information to their own personal frame of reference. An extreme form of letting expectations about others determine communication content is found in *stereotyping*. For example, many people expect the mentally retarded to be completely helpless. Excessive reliance on the most minute explanations (no matter how well-meant our intentions) may *force* the retarded individual to respond in such a way that he appears helpless, and in the process our stereotype is confirmed. Further, it does not seem inconsistent to people who harbor this stereotype that "normal" people can learn by making mistakes, but the retarded apparently cannot.* An extreme

---

*We are reminded of a story which took place at a picnic for mentally retarded students. The executive-director of the school took great pains to show one of the retarded students how to light up one of the barbecues—even to the point of demonstrating how to strike a match. The student replied: "I may be retarded, but I'm not stupid." All of us, are of course, guilty at times of holding on to stereotypes, even in the face of conflicting evidence that our stereotypes are wrong.

instance of stereotyping is found in the tendency to accept without question communications about things with which we agree, and to reject completely those things with which we are in complete disagreement. This tendency to ignore the "greys" and to react in "black or white" terms is called the "halo effect." Like stereotyping in general, it can be highly maladaptive in failing to make appropriate discriminations between the "good" and the "bad" which are intermixed in most situations.

Selectively Filtering Information which Conflicts with Our Present Beliefs: Most people resist change. The primary reason for this appears to be that we have to adopt new and often untried approaches with which we are unfamiliar. Sometimes, unfortunately, our filters work so efficiently that we exclude information which would have been highly beneficial to us. This is tantamount to putting on "emotional blinders" in that we persist in behaviors which may be clearly inappropriate or dysfunctional. Communications in this situation, are likely to have little effect, because they run counter to what we presently believe to be true.

Semantics (Words mean different things to different people): Language is a method of using symbols to represent facts and feelings. Strictly speaking we can't convey *meaning*; all we can do is convey *words*. But words may suggest quite different meanings for different people. For example, a workshop manager may state that efficiency is essential if the workshop is to survive. His interpretation of "efficiency" may include the means by which the workshop can buy new equipment, expand, and increase the present client-system by providing new jobs. But to handicapped employees, the word "efficiency" may suggest that the workshop is to undergo a "speed-up" with efficiency experts, time and motion specialists and the like, exerting close or tight supervision over the employee's job. In short, any attempt to communicate about efficiency must surmount the barrier of established meanings associated with the word.

The problem of semantics is particularly prevalent among the numerous professionals and clinical people in the rehabilitation field. Certain terms are used to describe specific situations (or people), and are often compounded into complex "in-languages" which rapidly become incomprehensible to outsiders. Unless one is aware of the *precise* definition of the terminology used, communication can quickly reach an impasse. Other professions, of course, face the same problems, and indicate the desirability of adopting a more common language which could help to alleviate this communication barrier.

NONVERBAL COMMUNICATION AND EMOTIONAL STATES: In trying to understand what a mentally retarded employee is trying to say to us (and thus to predict his or her future behavior) we often must draw upon many cues besides language. Facial gestures and bodily posture may tell us more about what the other person really thinks than the words he or she uses. Unfortunately, we ourselves often communicate things in the same manner unintentionally. Impatience with things over which we have little or no control often manifests itself into personal anger which may be further interpreted by an already sensitive worker as dissatisfaction with his work.

Further, workers who feel insecure, worried, or fearful, often conjure up all kinds of meanings to explain perfectly ordinary situations. For example, moving an employee off one job to another (without a careful explanation as to the reason) may carry with it a high degree of personal risk or threat for the employee concerned. Attempts to communicate with the employee when he is in this state of arousal, may be shut off completely.

While the above barriers to communication are far from exhaustive, they tend to cross most of the interpersonal processes which distort or block communication from taking place. We turn now to techniques for overcoming these barriers and improving the communication process.

TECHNIQUES FOR IMPROVED COMMUNICATION

Among other things, an effective communication system requires solving simultaneously two quite different problems. At a point in time, a manager must learn to improve his *transmis-*

sion (the words, ideas, and feelings he sends to the other person). Concurrently, the manager must cope with his *own reception* (his perception(s) of the other person's reactions to the communication). We shall devote the rest of this section to a discussion of several ways by which a manager can maximize his success in communicating with others.

UTILIZING FEEDBACK: Probably the single most important method of improving communication is through *feedback*. Technically, this term refers to the ability of a system to check on its own performance and to make corrections where necessary.† We frequently use this technique without being aware of it. For example, a good supervisor is alert for cues as to whether or not he is being understood. A mentally retarded employee who is highly excitable or confused gives off signals which tell the workshop manager that he must proceed carefully. The most critical feature of feedback is that it be *reciprocal*. It is important to be aware of not only the receiver's cues, but also the sender's. In this way, we are provided with a constant check on reality.

USING FACE-TO-FACE COMMUNICATION: In most situations direct, personal, (face-to-face) communications are preferable over other forms. The major reason for this is that the receiver and the sender can engage in immediate feedback. A skillful manager, for instance, can gauge how people are reacting to what he is saying, and modify his approach where necessary. Printed material doesn't allow for these shifts in emphasis and more often than not cannot convey the very personal nuances possible only through the human voice. This should not be interpreted to mean, however, that written messages have no place in organizations. Instructional material should be put in writing so that the employee to whom they are addressed can study them at leisure. The air of formality that written communications take on can be important also, in that we may wish to establish precedent and avoid ambiguous situations where each employee interprets rules and regulations for himself.

---

† For a sophisticated analysis of how principles of electronic communications may be applied to human communications, see N. Wiener, *Cybernetics* (Cambridge, Technology Press, 1954).

Ideally, both approaches (oral and written) should be used wherever possible. This would allow for more direct questions and answers by the parties involved and possible adjustments to meet any objections which arise. Once general agreement has been reached, the new procedure can be reduced to writing for future reference.

SENSITIVITY OR EMPATHY TO THE RECEIVER'S FRAME OF REFERENCE: It would be difficult to think of any organization which even begins to approach the enormous complexity present in the workshop setting with respect to sensitivity. Workshop managers must frequently work with a variety of client-systems (mentally retarded, physically handicapped, alcoholic placements, etc.) who exhibit wide differences in backgrounds and experiences. If a workshop manager wants to communicate with a mentally retarded employee, for example, he must find a way of (a) fitting his remarks to the individual's attitudes and beliefs, (b) making an appeal which is relevant to the employee's needs (which are often quite different from other employees), and (c) constantly checking (via feedback) to see that his message is being received and understood.

With respect to narrowing the gap of misunderstanding and heightening sensitivity to handicapped employees, we feel that sensitivity training (T-groups) sessions hold real promise. Confrontation, leveling, and similar interpersonal approaches have been shown to be highly successful in resolving problems which arise from individual differences. (We refer our reader to Ch. 6—OD and the Workshop—for a discussion of sensitivity training and other techniques.)

USING DIRECT, SIMPLE LANGUAGE: A message (whether verbal or nonverbal) should be as straightforward and as logically stated as possible. A frequently recurring problem in communications is that we attempt to include or convey too many ideas at the same time. This situation can become intensified when we consider severely mentally retarded workers, and requires special care to avoid the confusion which results from the transmission of multiple messages.

Finally, even among professionals in the field, each manager should attempt to insure that his announcements, public statements, and policy directives are couched in clear, direct language. Avoidance of wordy and needlessly complicated jargon can help to overcome this situation.

Having briefly outlined some of the major techniques toward more effective communication, we will conclude this chapter with a discussion of communication networks.

COMMUNICATION NETWORKS AND INFORMATION CHANNELS

A communication network is a term used to describe a specific arrangement (or configuration) of information channels. Typically, we view organizations as having a vertical communication channel (superior-subordinate) and a horizontal communication channel (across departmental or functional lines). These two dimensions are frequently referred to as the formal communication structure, and are graphically pictured in the organization chart. Clearly, the formal communication structure is only one part of an organization's capacity to disseminate information through its various levels. Informal methods, such as the "grapevine" and "rumor outlets" play an equally important role, and must be considered along with the formal system.

An interesting series of experiments utilizing different communication networks was conducted by Alex Bavelas in 1950.[4] The only form of communication allowed was by means of written notes which were passed to one another. The subjects in these experiments were isolated and put to work on a task while the experimenter controlled and manipulated four different communication patterns or *nets* (networks). (See Fig. 10.)

Central to Bavelas' research was the assumption that the distance between any two people in a network was one. Communications between the five people in each net could take place only through the channels indicated in Figure 10. For

---

[4] A. Bavelas, "Communication Patterns in Task-Oriented Groups," in D. Cartwright and A. Zander, eds., *Group Dynamics* (New York, Harper & Row, 1960).

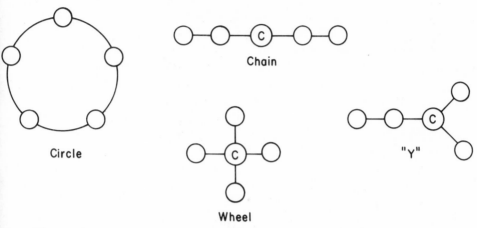

Figure 10. Examples of Communication Nets

example, in the circle, notes could be passed in either direction (left or right). In the wheel only "C" could communicate with all four others. In the circle, all positions were equally central, while in the wheel only "C" was central.

Using different problems (which ranged from very simple to very complex) a number of conclusions were reached about the relative effectiveness and level of satisfaction experienced in the various nets.

1. Wheel groups required less time to solve simple problems, while circle groups solved more complex problems faster. (Availability of information appears to be the key to the solution of simple problems, *providing* the problem can be solved by anyone in the net; with complex problems, a full range of intellectual resources is better because of the nature of the problem.)

2. The greater the degree of participation, the higher the level of satisfaction. (People in the circle net expressed greater satisfaction and positive feelings about membership than in any other net.)

3. The likelihood of emerging as a leader increases with the centrality (position "C" in each net) of one's position.

The implications of these conclusions for the workshop are as follows: (a) where the task is relatively simple, such as sorting clothing into sizes, it would be desirable to adopt a wheel, "Y," or a chain; (b) where the task is relatively more complex, such as appliance renovation or furniture reconstruction, it would probably be better to use a circle. The rationale here, is that the task is likely to permit more exceptions, feature unique sub-problems, and be more unstructured in nature. Obviously, these are only general inferences, as the level of morale of the employees or the individual need satisfactions each worker expects to receive from the task may take precedence over efficiency.

Up to this point (Ch. 1 through Ch. 8), we have concerned ourselves principally with *process*. The remaining chapters will deal with more global considerations, which are for the most part *structural* in nature.

THE ORGANIZATION/ENVIRONMENT IN-

TERFACE:

CONSIDERATIONS OF STRUCTURE AND

DESIGN

F OR THE LARGER PART of this text, we have been examining the interdependencies and processes *within* the organization. We now turn our attention to another set of interdependencies the organization must face: those brought about by the organization/environment interface. We concern ourselves primarily with the effect of this interface on structural design of the organization in this chapter; review technological considerations in the following chapter; and conclude the discussion of this interface with a chapter on Management Information Systems in the workshop.

There have been numerous discussions about which form of structural design is the most appropriate in the rehabilitation workshop setting. Nelson* suggests that in consideration of the "operational duality" (the processing of human and business inputs in order to achieve workshop goals associated with each of these areas), a "balanced Organization Chart" or structure must be achieved. His interpretation of this "balance" leads to functional divisionalization along the lines of "professional services" and "business services," as shown on page 76.

---

*The discussion of "operational duality" and "organizational balance" can be found in N. Nelson, *Workshop for the Handicapped in the United States: A Historical and Developmental Perspective* (Springfield, Charles C Thomas Publisher, 1971), pp. 337-363.

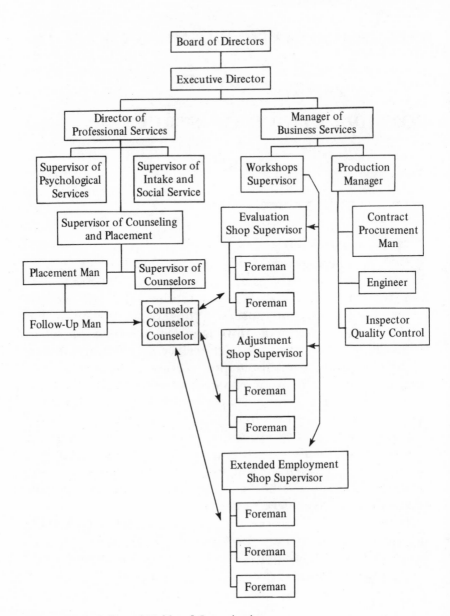

Figure 11. A Balanced Table of Organization

It is evident that the service and business components are functionally separated, so that both parts of the "operational duality" should theoretically deal effectively with their sometimes divergent goals.

Yet is this structure appropriate to all workshops? Should the administrator divisionalize by function, or is product (or project) divisionalization more effective? Should branch operations be subject to centralized decision making, or would decentralization of operations result in better decisions?

We believe that some tentative answers to many of these important questions can be developed through a review of current empirical research, which indicates that certain structural "styles" may be more appropriate than others, depending on the situational factors presented by the environment and the technologies employed by the organization. It is not our intent to take issue with Nelson's approach regarding organizational structure, nor is it our intent to demonstrate what the appropriate structure might be under each environmental setting, but rather it is our wish to provide some "food for thought" for administrators who must face the myriad structural questions concerning effective administration of workshops.

THE SYSTEMS APPROACH EXPANDED

In order to allow us to analyze environmental situations further, we find it necessary to expand the explanation of the processes of input, throughput, and output within the organizational system. It is evident from Figure 12 (page 78) that both input and output sub-environments can be further broken into five components: (1) capital or money flow, (2) material flow (raw material on the input side and finished on the output side), (3) people (both handicapped and non-handicapped), (4) orders (receiving of contracts on the input side, and purchases on the output side), and (5) information flows[1] (which will be treated more extensively in the chapter on Management Information Systems).

---

[1] Nelson *Workshop for the Handicapped in the United States: A Historical and Developmental Perspective*, p. 360.

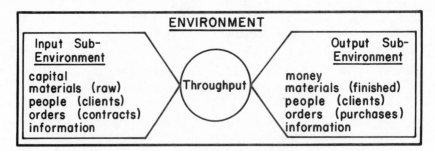

Figure 12. Environmental Process and the Organizational System

As noted in Figure 12 it is during the input-output processes of the organizational system that the organization/environment interface occurs. It is at these points that the environment imposes constraints and contingencies upon the system. What is the nature of these constraints and contingencies?

On the input side we find: (1) that raw materials may become hard to acquire because of shortages in the environment or because of prohibitively high costs, (2) contract orders may fall off because of a declining economy, discontinuations of product lines, or new technologies that are developed, (3) capital may be hard to come by because of changes in national fiscal policy, or because sales did not reach expectations, (4) client referrals may increase or decrease in unanticipated amounts because of shifts in external agencies' policies, and (5) information may be misleading or false, leading to erroneous or disastrous decisions.

On the output side, we may face various other problems: (1) finished materials may be overstocked causing layoffs and excess costs, or finished materials may be understocked, causing losses in both customers and income, (2) job availability may be poor for clients ready for entry into the labor market because of increased unemployment or reluctance on the part of the community to hire the handicapped, (3) completed contracts may never be reimbursed because of "insolvency" of the contracting company, (4) sales or other income may not meet expected or budgeted figures, causing expenses to exceed revenues and threatening a "crisis" situation, and (5) information about workshop activity presented to the public may actually be harmful.

A further point is the interdependency of the input and output variables. For example, poor information about sales and/or donations (inputs) may materially affect production and inventories of raw materials (input), as well as finished material inventories (output).

Faced with these contingencies and constraints, what alternatives can the workshop utilize to cope with this environmental "penetration" into its system? The following section will outline some of the alternatives available.

Co-optation can be described as incorporating that part of the environment causing problems into the organization, in order to better cope with it. A common form of co-optation within the workshop setting is to select certain individuals (such as lawyers) for board positions in order to make use of special expertise in dealing with problems which arise. Another example would be the inclusion of a union leader to avoid conflict with the union when bidding for contracts in which the union might be involved.

A second alternative available to the organization facing high levels of environmental contamination would be to *succumb* to the environment. The most severe instance of succumbing would be to close the workshop because of an inability to meet expenses, or an inability to continue to justify the workshop's existence. Other directions that this alternative might take are: removing the organization from those parts of the environment it cannot effectively deal with; refusing to recognize the environment at that point, or rationing of resources.

In any event, we view this second alternative as the least desirable, and consider it dysfunctional as it could conceivably lead to eventual closing of the workshop.

NEUTRALIZING AND UTILIZING THE ENVIRONMENT

All successful organizations learn to accept and anticipate the environment and capitalize on it. Since this approach views the environment as an open-system in which organizational action determines to a great extent its success, it is the most desirable alternative in our opinion, and will for that reason be analyzed in greater detail.

In order to operationalize this approach we turn our attention to methods of implementing neutralization and utilization of the environment. Possibly the most important contributor to this theoretical notion is Thompson.[2] The following methods are his conclusions regarding successful adaption of the organization to its environment.

BUFFERING: This method can be described as "padding" the organization from the environmental shocks. Some examples of buffering on the input side of the organization system are: (1) maintaining an employee/client "pool" so as not to be caught when a production spot is vacated due to client placement or termination, (2) maintaining a "safety" stock of materials so that shortages don't adversely affect production capabilities, and (3) maintenance of a savings account to use in case of unanticipated expenditures such as uninsured loss.

On the output side, buffering is most evident in the inventories built up to meet sales that may be higher than expected.

LEVELING: A second method of neutralizing the environment is leveling. Whereas buffering is intended to absorb the environmental shocks, leveling is utilized to smooth out the fluctuations in the environment.

All workshops face certain times of the year that are more predictable than others with regard to employment. In workshops which do *not* plan for these fluctuations, it is typical to find hiring during the "fast" seasons and lay-offs during the "slow" seasons. In order to better smooth out these peaks and valleys, the organization should consider various methods of leveling.

On the input side, leveling may take the form of encouraging donations in typically poor donation months, by increasing levels of public service announcements and public relations.

On the output side, leveling can be implemented through

---

[2] J. D. Thompson, *Organizations in Action* (New York, McGraw-Hill, 1967), pp. 19-24.

various "specials" offered to customers and/or the figuring of bids for contract purposes yielding less of a margin of return. (It must be pointed out, however, that this has proved fatal to some workshops and should be adopted with extreme caution.)

ADAPTING: The final method of utilizing or neutralizing the environment is adapting to it. This is a very important method, as in most cases, neither buffering, leveling, nor a combination of the two, can adequately eliminate all of the environmental "penetration."

In our opinion, the most effective and successful way of adapting to the environment is through careful structural design of the organization. When structural design is done with consideration of the degree of penetration by the environment into the organizational system, it can be a very valuable tool for adaptation. On the other hand, when structural design is accomplished without consideration of environmental penetration, dysfunctional organizational behavior is a likely result.

In order to more fully understand the notion of environmental "penetration" into the organizational system, we will turn our attention to a conceptualization of environment.

DYNAMIC AND STABLE ENVIRONMENTS: A QUESTION OF PENETRATION

For analytical purposes, we will use an environmental construct proposed by Burns and Stalker.† In their study of twenty firms in the United Kingdom, they found it useful to characterize the environment as being either dynamic or stable. The determination of dynamism was the degree of uncertainty that was faced by the firm. In other words, the higher the level of uncertainty, the more dynamic the environment in which the firm's organizational system had to survive. It seems likely that one of the problems associated with this form of conceptualization, would be the determination of the degree to which uncertainty is present.

---

†For a more complete treatment see T. Burns and G. M. Stalker, *Management of Innovation* (London, Tavistock Publishings).

In order to cope with this situation, a scheme was proposed by two American researchers (Lawrence and Lorsch‡) who attempted to replicate some of the findings suggested by Burns and Stalker. These authors devised a questionnaire that was administered to determine the perceived uncertainty in an environment. Total uncertainty is a factor of three elements:

1. *The clarity of the information received from the environment*—In other words, is the information valid and reliable? The more reliable and valid the information, the greater degree of certainty and, therefore, stability. The less reliable and certain, the higher degree of uncertainty.

2. *The certainty of the cause/effect relationships*—The greater the knowledge the organization has of the different interrelationships taking place in the environment, the higher the degree of certainty. The less they know about these interrelationships, the greater the degree of uncertainty.

3. *The greater the time span of feedback*—The longer it takes to get feedback from the environment, the greater the uncertainty, and therefore, the more dynamic an environment, and vice versa.

The combination of these three elements gives the total level of uncertainty and degree of dynamism in the organizational environment. Figure 13 expresses this dynamism graphically.

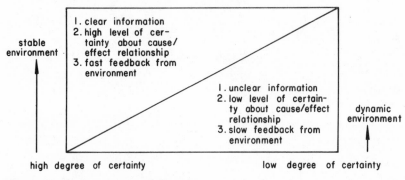

Figure 13. Environment and Certainty

---

‡For the complete questionnaire see P. R. Lawrence and J. W. Lorsch, "Methodological Appendix," *Organizational and Environment: Managing Differentiation and Integration* (Boston, Harvard Publications, 1967), pp. 247-268.

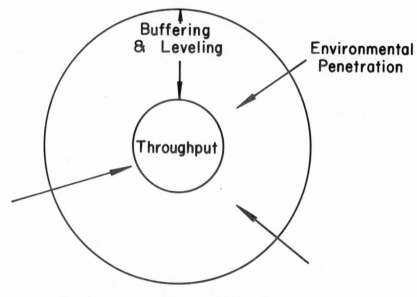

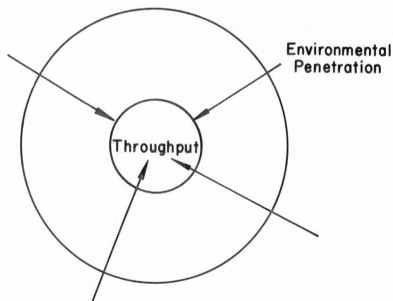

Figure 14. Stable Environments

In a stable environment, penetration does not often pierce the buffering and leveling zones of the organization enough to reach the throughput stage, while in a dynamic environment, penetration succeeds in reaching and disturbing the throughput process.

While many of the conclusions reached by Lawrence and Lorsch are beyond the scope of this text, we feel that most administrators could utilize the above mentioned elements to better analyze the dynamism of their own environments on a subjective basis. In order to operationalize these concepts, the administrator might question whether his information was timely and accurate; whether he felt confident in the information he received; and whether he felt the information was an accurate reflection of what was actually happening. If the administrator answered *no* to all or a majority of these questions, then he is most likely facing an environment that tends more toward dynamism than to stability.

Returning to the ideas of neutralization and utilization by buffering, leveling and/or adapting to the environment, it seems both logical and consistent to the authors that since each of these methods are in essence protective "skins" enclosing the throughput process, the higher the level of uncertainty (and, therefore, dynamism in the environment), the greater the degree of "penetration' into these protective elements of the organization. A review of Figures 13 and 14 illustrate the degree of penetration under stable and dynamic conditions.

In order to understand our treatment of structural design under low and high degrees of penetration (stable or dynamic environments), we will first review how the classical and human relations school of management treated the problems of structure.

SOME PRESCRIPTIVE METHODS OF STRUCTURAL DESIGN

Rather than treat each of the various sub-schools of classical management thought, we will, in the interest of brevity, outline methods of structural design common to all of the various schools. The traditionalists believed that the answer to the structural question was: (1) to departmentalize by functions (sales, production, etc.), (2) to specialize these functions within departments, and (3) to standardize tasks by assigning rules and/or repetitive procedures to carry them out. Coordination of the various department's functions was not felt to be a problem because the hierarchial structure of the organization was considered to be appropriate in all instances.

As indicated in the first few chapters of this text, the human relations school developed because of the felt inadequacies of the classical school of managerial thought. Under this school's direction, emphasis on structural design was removed from considerations of the formal structure to that of the informal organization. Under this approach, consideration of motivation, values, and attitudes were primary to the development of participative management. Decentralized decision-making processes were expounded to encourage the individual to attain his self-realization needs. To accomplish these goals, a plea was made to keep the organizational structure "loose." In this way it was felt the organization could best realize its objectives.

Although each of these schools handled the design of the organization in a somewhat dichotomous manner, both of the approaches were prescriptive in that each school felt that their method was the best way to solve the structural problems of the organization for all situations.

It is interesting to note that two such apparently dichotomous methods frequently existed side by side in management thought and philosophy. One well might ask, "How is this possible?" We feel that the answer comes from the empirical evidence present in a systems viewpoint of the environment-organization interface and its effect on structure. This systems viewpoint is called *contingency theory* and its development and implications will monopolize the remainder of the discussion in this chapter.

CONTINGENCY THEORY APPROACH TO STRUCTURAL DESIGN

Contingency theory at the organizational-environment interface does not prescribe the best way to design the organization, but rather states that structure is *contingent upon* or *dependent upon* the environment situation it is dealing with. In other words, the appropriateness of any type of structural design (including those prescriptive methods of the traditionalists or behaviorists) is dependent on the degree of penetration by the environment. In order to understand this relationship, we will examine more thoroughly two studies cited earlier in this chapter.

As mentioned earlier, Tom Burns and G. M. Stalker conceptualized the environment as being either dynamic or stable. Of far greater importance than this conceptualization was the finding that different management styles and different organizational structures tend to be more successful under each of these two situations. With a stable environment (low environmental penetration), the most successful firms utilized a *mechanistic* style of management while those firms that were the most successful in the dynamic environment (high level of environmental penetration), were the firms that employed *organic* management systems and organizational structures.

A *mechanistic* management system is appropriate to stable conditions. It is characterized by:

a. the specialized differentiation of functional tasks into which the problems and tasks facing the concern as a whole are broken down.

b. the abstract nature of each individual task, which is pursued with techniques and purposes more or less distinct from those of the concern as a whole; i.e. the functionaries tend to pursue the technical improvement of means, rather than the accomplishment of the ends of the concern.

c. the reconciliation, for each level in the hierarchy, of these distinct performances by the immediate supervisors, who are also, in turn, responsible for seeing that each is relevant in his own special part of the main task.

d. the precise definition of rights and obligations and technical methods attached to each functional role.

e. the translation of rights and obligations and methods into the responsibilities of a functional position.

f. hierarchial structure of control, authority and communication.

g. a reinforcement of the hierarchial structure by the location of knowledge of actualities exclusively at the top of the hierarchy, where the final reconciliation of distinct tasks and assessment of relevance is made.

h. a tendency for interaction between the members of the concern to be vertical, i.e. between superior and subordinate.

i. a tendency for operations and working behavior to be governed by the instructions and decisions issued by superiors.

j. insistence on loyalty to the concern and obedience to superiors as a condition of membership.

k. a greater importance and prestige attaching to internal (local) rather than to general (cosmopolitan) knowledge.[3]

The *organic* form is appropriate to changing conditions, which give rise constantly to fresh problems and unforeseen requirements for action. It is characterized by:

a. the contributive nature of special knowledge and experience to a common task of the concern.

b. the "realistic" nature of the individual task, which is seen as set by the total situation of the concern.

c. the adjustment and continual re-definition of individual tasks through interaction with others.

d. the shedding of "responsibility" as a limited field of rights, obligations and methods. (Problems may not be posted upwards, downwards or sideways as being someone else's responsibility).

e. the spread of the commitment to the concern beyond any technical definition.

f. a network structure of control, authority, and communication. The sanctions which apply to the individual's conduct in his working role derive more from presumed community of interest with the rest of the working organization in the survival and growth of the firm, and less from a contractual relationship between himself and a non-personal corporation, represented for him by an immediate superior.

g. omniscience no longer imputed to the head of the concern; knowledge about the technical or commercial nature of the here and now task may be located anywhere in the network; this location becoming the *ad hoc* center of control authority and communication.

h. a lateral rather than a vertical direction of communication through the organization, communication between people of different rank, also, resembling consultation rather than command.

i. a content of communication which consists of information and advice rather than instructions and decisions.

j. commitment to the concern's tasks and to the "technological ethos" of material progress and expansion is more highly valued than loyalty and obedience.

k. importance and prestige attach to affiliations and expertise valid in the industrial and technical and commercial milieux external to the firm.[4]

---

[3] Burns and Stalker, *Management of Innovation*, pp. 119-122.
[4] Burns and Stalker, *Management of Innovation*, pp. 119-122.

A review of these systems reveal some interesting points. In the stable environment, where environmental penetration is low, we find that the most successful system is the *mechanistic*, which parallels the *classical* approach closely.

On the other hand, in the dynamic environment, where penetration is high, the *organic system of management* (which parallels the human relationists approach) is more effective.

One of the more important implications of the research findings is that the classical and human relations approach can coexist because each is appropriate under different environmental situations. The greater the environmental penetration, the more successful a firm is likely to be by employing an *organic* system, while under conditions of low environmental penetration, the more successful firm is likely to employ a *mechanistic* form of structure.

With this research as background into the contingency approach to structure, we now turn to an expanded version of this approach.

CONTINGENCY THEORY REVISITED

Paul Lawrence and Jay Lorsch, building on the notions of the mechanistic and organic systems of management style proposed by Burns and Stalker, developed their *Contingency Theory of Organizations*. As mentioned previously, this research and its findings are beyond the scope of this text. We will explore only those aspects that apply to the design of organizational structure.

The primary purpose of the research was to determine whether environments that could be characterized as having rapid rates of change and high degrees of uncertainty would produce different demands on organizations than environments which could be characterized as having low degrees of uncertainty (high certainty) and low rates of change. Firms from three industrial environments (dynamic, stable, and intermediate) were examined in order to determine whether the characteristics of successful firms were noticeably different than the less successful.

A related question was the determination of whether or not differing degrees of dynamism in each environment dictated different characteristics of successful firms *between* each of the environments.

The authors discovered that two concepts were critical to their analytical framework; differentiation, and integration (or put more simply, specialization and coordination). Firms that were found to be the most successful in the dynamic environment had high degrees of both structural differentiation and integration, while successful firms in stable environments had less differentiation and integration. The significance of these findings are as follows:

> ... administrators in higher performing organizations developed behavior patterns and organizational practices which enabled them effectively to manage the two essential organizational states of differentiation and integration in accordance with the demands of their particular environment. In the most dynamic environment . . . the effective businesses had organizations in which the managers of several functional departments had developed highly differentiated patterns of thought and behavior in relation to the demands of their dynamic environments. In the more stable industry . . . the effective organization had functional departments with less differentiation between them. . . . The effective organization in the third environment studied . . . had achieved a state of differentiation which fell between the extremes represented by the (other) organizations (studied). The effective organizations also achieved the required state of interdepartmental integration or collaboration. The less effective organizations in each environment failed to achieve the required state of differentiation and/or integration, and thus had difficulty meeting the demands of their environment.[5]

IMPLICATIONS OF SITUATIONAL RESEARCH ON ORGANIZATIONAL DESIGN

Having reviewed a brief survey of the research findings of Burns and Stalker and Lawrence and Lorsch, it should be

---

[5] Lawrence and Lorsch, "Methodological Appendix," *Organizational and Environment: Managing Differentiation and Integration*, pp. 2-3 of abstract.

evident that structural design cannot be determined arbitrarily by the application of prescriptive methods to each and every situation, but rather that *situational analysis* is needed to determine which structure will be the most successful, given the degree of environmental penetration.

Applying these findings to the questions raised at the beginning of this chapter, it appears that functional divisionalization (mechanistic management style) will be more effective and appropriate where environmental penetration is low, while project or product divisionalization (organic management style) is more appropriate under conditions of high levels of environmental penetration.

Another implication that may be drawn is that decentralized decision making and structure is likely to be much more effective in situations where there is high environmental penetration.

Though still other implications for structural design may be suggested, we leave these to the reader to develop depending on the particular situation he faces. We will now turn our attention to some technological considerations and their implications on organizational design.

Chapter 10

TECHNOLOGICAL CONSIDERATIONS IN

A CLIENT-CENTERED SYSTEM

APPROACHES TO TECHNOLOGICAL CONSIDERATIONS

MUCH DISCUSSION IN THE PAST few decades has been devoted to the effects of technology on man, society, and the work ethic. Because many of these topics deal with changing human values, problems of alienation and depersonalization, the potential effects of increased leisure time, and presumed invasions on personal privacy,* we find it fashionable to look upon technology as an enemy, and find ourselves inputting magical powers to many of the technological processes.

Although each of the above topics provide provocative material from which to approach a chapter (or book, for that matter), we will instead set as our goal the presentation of some basic considerations dealing with technological processes in a client-centered system.

In order to operationalize this goal, we will examine three technological typologies. The first typology will align itself with an overview of technological processes. The remaining two typologies will develop classifications of technology by: (a) processes employed by the organization and (b) the perceived knowledge of the client and the rehabilitative processes.

TECHNOLOGY DEFINED

Although many definitions of technology could be utilized, we find it desirable to accept the definition provided by Perrow

---

*For interesting discussions on each of these topics, the reader may refer to J. G. Burke, *The New Technology and Human Values* (Belmont, Wadsworth Publishing Co., 1966).

who feels that technology is: "a means of transforming raw materials (human, symbolic, or material) into desirable goods and services."†

This conceptualization allows us to separate man and machines from the *total* technological process, and is internally consistent with our concept of the organization as a system. Technology, so defined, provides the link between the input and output processes:

> ... technology is required, not only in the actual production process, but also for procuring the inputs of materials, capital, and labor and disposing of the output to some other organization or consumer, and for coordinating the three "functions" or "phases" in input-transformation-output.[1]

A NOTE ON TECHNOLOGICAL TYPOLOGIES

Scott and Mitchell, in their review of technological typologies, feel that it is fruitful to review various technological systems based on research done in manufacturing firms, because:

1. manufacturing is still the focal activity of industrial nations.
2. research in their (manufacturing firms) technological processes may provide valuable conceptual clues for the analysis of the technologies of nonmanufacturing organizations.[2]

These authors stress, however, that typologies developed from studies in manufacturing firms "present severe limitations to their usefulness as theoretical models,"[3] for non-manufacturing firms, or firms employing client-centered technological systems. While we share the concern of model transferability expressed by these authors, and accept this as a

---

† A more complete definition of technology may be found in C. Perrow, *Organizational Analysis: A Sociological View* (Belmont, Brooks/Cole Publishing Co., 1970).

[1] Perrow, *Organizational Analysis: A Sociological View*, p. 75.

[2] W. G. Scott and T. R. Mitchell, *Organizational Theory: A Structural and Behavioral Analysis* (Homewood, Irwin-Dorsey Limited, 1972), p. 238.

[3] *Ibid.*

limitation, we still feel it both necessary and desirable to draw some conclusions from current empirical research concerning parallel situations confronted in client-centered systems.

AN OVERVIEW OF TECHNOLOGICAL PROCESSES

J. D. Thompson‡ in examining variations in technology, takes a general approach which envisions technological processes in the light of problems encountered with the customer (client) served. Thompson's model identified three separate and distinct classifications: long-linked, mediating, and intensive.

Long-Linked Technologies

Long-Linked technologies employ a sequential or serial interdependence of several acts or events in order to accomplish the desired outcome in product or service. The best example of long-linked technology would be the automobile assembly line, where act A (attaching the body to the frame) must be performed before act B (putting doors on body) could be accomplished. (See Fig. 15.)

Figure 15. Long-Linked Technology

Although this process is generally more applicable to manufacturing firms, it is being used in a modified sense in many client-centered programs. An example of this would be where each client is processed through a sequentially designed program over a specified period of time. Typically, this could take the form of a medical check, aptitude testing, dexterity testing,

---

‡ It is doubtful that a more complete theoretical model has been developed than that proposed by J. D. Thompson, *Organizations in Action* (New York, McGraw-Hill Publishing Co., 1967).

etc. The most important point here is that each stage (activity) of the program is highly interdependent upon the preceding stage.

For the most part, problems encountered when this technological process is used are largely those caused by inefficient scheduling of events. Therefore, planning takes on extreme importance if this process is to be successful.

Mediating Technologies

Organizations which employ this technological process provide a link between the customer and the client. One of the best examples of this technology is the vocationally oriented, rehabilitation workshop, which brings together a customer (community employer) with a client skilled in the appropriate vocational trade desired by the employer. (See Fig. 16.)

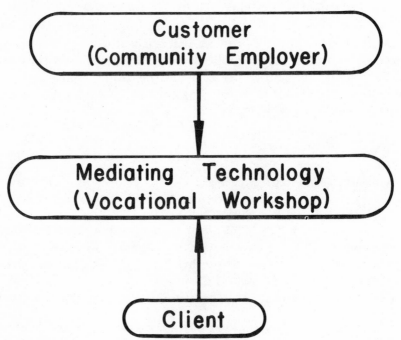

Figure 16. Mediating Technology

Major problems encountered by the facility employing this process arise from the customer's desire to obtain a standardized product (client). For example, a community employer who utilizes the facility's services by hiring a client trained as a welder will expect each client hired to have knowledge of the basic processes of that trade. If the employer is successful in procuring a client who does well in the work, he will not only measure future clients on the basis of acquired skills, but will also expect others to do equally as well. This *leveling* process tends to ignore the importance of individual differences.

Intensive Technologies

The final classification in Thompson's technological scheme is intensive technology. In this process, a variety of techniques and special skills are utilized in order to achieve a desired outcome in the finished material (human, symbolic, or material). When the raw material is human, intensive technologies are often regarded as therapeutic in nature.

One of the best examples of this technological process in a client-centered system would be a hospital emergency wing. Here, different combinations of services, such as nurses, dieticians, specialized practitioners, and post-operative specialists (occupational therapists, social workers, and/or rehabilitation counselors) may be provided, depending on the nature of the accident or illness sustained by the client (See Fig. 17).

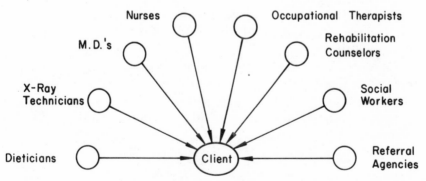

Figure 17. Various Available Professional Skills and Services

Since an intensive technology is custom designed to each client's needs, problems which may occur are:
1. lack of ability to provide these specialized services for a particular client.
2. picking the appropriate combination of skills and/or specialists.

TECHNOLOGY AND STRUCTURE

Joan Woodward's research into technological processes and their implications for organizational structure must be included among the most rigorous. Focusing on manufacturing environments and the successful technological system employed within each, her project included approximately 100 firms in the United Kingdom and lasted over 10 years.§

Although 11 classifications for production systems were identified in this research, Woodward found it convenient to subsume them under three major classes: (1) unit and small batch, (2) large batch and mass production, and (3) continuous process production systems.

Unit and Small Batch Production Systems

Firms utilizing this technological process, considered to be the least complex, are often identified as job-order firms or "custom builders." Most of the products tend to be heterogeneous (or one-of-a-kind) and the problems that occur are largely nonrepetitive.

Organizations that employ craftsmen (such as cabinet makers) or deal with non-repetitive problems in which only a few copies of a product are actually produced (such as missle components firms) frequently employ this technological method.

---

§*See J. Woodward, Industrial Organization: Theory and Practice* (London, Oxford University Press, 1965).

Large Batch and Mass Production Systems

This production system differs from the small batch system, in that it does not necessarily produce only to order, but also maintains an inventory for anticipated orders. The products are usually made from parts which share a common mold or repetitive process and are relatively standardized upon completion.

Examples of this technological process parallel those described under long-linked technologies developed earlier, with coordination and scheduling of activities the main attendant problems.

Continuous Production Processing

Firms utilizing this process (which is the most complex of the technological processes) have typically long production runs and completely standardized products. Although oil refineries and chemical producers are the best examples of this type of technology, many firms which produce drugs and other pharmaceutical products also fall into this category.

Since many of the production processes in this category are completely automated and changeovers to new methods may be extremely costly; marketing of products, anticipation of demand, and proper scheduling of production runs play extremely important roles under this technological process.

WOODWARD'S RESEARCH FINDINGS

While Woodward's research indicated many important findings relative to technology and structure, we will review only those that are germane and of interest to the workshop setting:

1. the greater the complexity of the production system (on an increasing scale from unit to continuous process), the greater the number of levels of management
2. the greater the technological complexity of the produc-

tion system, the higher the ratio of supervisors to non-supervisory workers

3. the ratio of indirect to direct labor increased as technological complexity increased

4. staff personnel per worker increased from approximately 1 in 8 in unit production processes, to approximately 1 in 5 for large batch, and approximately 1 in 2 for continuous process systems

5. labor costs decreased as a percentage of total costs as the scale of complexity increased (This was so because of the increased use of automated systems which reduced the need for labor.)

IMPLICATIONS FOR THE WORKSHOP

If Woodward's research findings hold true for client-centered systems, we would expect to find that successful workshops which "process" clients on a unit basis, should have quite different structural compositions than those that "process" clients on a mass or continuous basis. Further, (as suggested by the findings) it is highly likely that each type of workshop will face different problems.

For example, facilities which "process" clients on a unit basis will find that most of their problems exist in the packaging of custom programs for each client. In order to deal effectively with design problems, staff members should, of necessity, be highly trained professionals who enjoy maximum contact with each client. This should be interpreted to mean that each professional should have a minimum case load.

On the other hand, facilities which "process" clients in large or mass production batches, will find that developing the actual sequential program for the clients to be the major problem area. Planning and scheduling will take up the bulk of the system's problems here, and it is likely that many of the staff members employed will deal with the programming problems, rather than with the actual client problems.

Finally, those facilities employing a continuous system of

processing clients will find that much of their problems lie in "selling" the finished product (the client) to make room for new clients in order to keep the system moving efficiently. For this reason, we might expect to find agencies or facilities dealing with continuous processing technologies adding to their "sales" ability by bringing placement and employment counselors into staff positions.

PROBLEMS OF MODEL TRANSFERABILITY

To the extent that the research findings and problem areas defined above for each facility employing the different production processes seem logically transferable to client-centered systems, the findings are useful. A major problem still exists, however, in determining whether a facility is actually utilizing a unit, large batch, or continuous process system. A logical and consistent method of determining *which* system should be employed is possible through examination of a third technological typology which examines: (a) the characteristics of the clients, and (b) the staffs' knowledge of the rehabilitative processes.

TECHNOLOGY—AN INTEGRATED APPROACH

In examining organizations utilizing people-changing technologies, Perrow distinguishes two important variables: (1) the nature of the raw material (whether or not it is understood) and (2) the degree of the raw material's variability (whether or not it is uniform).**

With slight modification (substituting "knowledge of the rehabilitative process" for "nature of the raw material," and "perceived characteristics of the client" for "the degree of variability"), we have developed four quadrants which we find useful in determining whether a facility "processes" its client in a unit, mass, or continuous process basis (See Fig. 18).

**See Perrow, *Organizational Analysis: A Sociological View*, pp. 73-99.

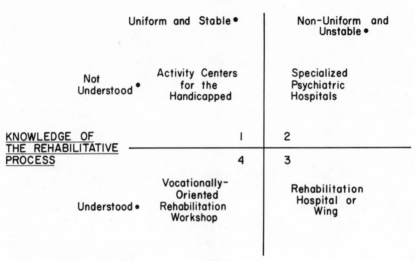

Figure 18. Perceived Characteristics of Client

Cell 1 identifies one of the numerous activity center programs for the handicapped. Here, the rehabilitative process may not be understood by the staff and each client may be viewed by the staff as sharing a common (or uniform) characteristic (e.g. mental retardation, cerebral palsy, or social retardation).

In cell 2 (the specialized psychiatric hospital), we often find that both the client and the appropriate rehabilitative process are considered by the staff as having elusive properties. Subsequently, each individual is treated differently and only an analysis of the individual's beliefs, values, and motives will give adequate information with which to try to custom design an appropriate rehabilitative program.

The best example of cell 3 (where the client is perceived as being nonuniform while the rehabilitative process is understood), may well be the rehabilitation hospital or wing. Although these programs may vary in nature (e.g individuals needing alcohol or drug de-toxification, or occupational or physical therapy after sustaining an injury or illness) the knowledge of the rehabilitative process may be well known for each situation. Each client, in this case, is considered nonuniform because each program may require different combinations of services depending on the diagnosed problems.

Cell 4 concerns itself with a vocationally-oriented, rehabilitation workshop. The client, in this system, is usually considered uniform (a handicapped individual in need of behavior modification or skills-training in order to secure gainful employment) and the rehabilitative processes perceived as understood (counseling and vocational training).

Relating back to the concepts of unit, large batch, and continuous process systems, we find it logical to assume that under conditions approximating cell 4, it is likely that the facility will employ a technology similar in nature to a continuous production process, with the attendant problems of "selling" the finished products (clients) in order to allow new clients into the program.

In those facilities which view the client as nonuniform and perceive the rehabilitative process as either understood or not understood (cells 2 and 3), a custom designed process would appear to be the appropriate choice in that the client's situation must be determined first before program design is considered.

Finally, if the client is viewed as uniform but the rehabilitative process is not understood (cell 1), a large batch system would most likely be the most effective form.

LIMITATIONS OF TECHNOLOGICAL IMPLICATIONS

It has not been our intent to determine the appropriateness of employing one technological process over any of the others defined in this chapter, as each may be equally appropriate depending on the values held and goals established by a particular facility's board of directors. What we have tried to suggest is that technological considerations and knowledge of the rehabilitative process are closely related. It seems logical to assume that client-centered systems which carefully consider the nature of these complex relationships (and plan accordingly) are in an infinitely superior position to cope with their environment than those that do not.

It must be pointed out, however, that although transferability of some of the findings from technological typologies developed in manufacturing firms to client-centered systems *seems* logical, this is only a tentative proposal at best. Further empirical research will be needed in order to verify the validity of such transferability.

One possible source of information toward better understanding the nature of the rehabilitation process lies in the facility's ability to assess the quality of the information it is receiving. The following chapter will describe the characteristics of a client-centered organization's management information system (MIS).

Chapter 11

MANAGEMENT INFORMATION SYSTEMS:

A STRUCTURAL APPROACH

THE CONCENTRATION IN the two previous chapters has been on the interdependencies between the workshop, the environment it interfaces with, and the technological processes it employs. We have seen that there is no perfect solution for all workshop situations, but rather that a particular management style employed and the organizational structure necessary for success is dependent or contingent upon the amount of environmental penetration and the complexity of the technology utilized. In effect, organizational structure and management style should be considered dependent variables.

Before abandoning the notion of environmental penetration and the consideration of technological processes, it is necessary to examine one further interdependent relationship, that of the structural design of the management information system (hereafter referred to as MIS). For, if management style and organizational structure are dependent upon the environmental situation and technological complexity, it would appear logical and consistent to assume that the design of the MIS directed at the successful transference of information for decision making is also dependent on the same variables. We feel that great insight into the nature of these relationships can be achieved by pursuing this line of thought, and will proceed accordingly.

MIS: A WORKING DEFINITION

As always, it is helpful to build some common points of reference for our reader. The following is our notion of information and information systems as we perceive them.

"Information is an occurrence or a set of occurrences which

carry messages, and, when received by the recipients via any of the senses, will increase their state of knowledge."[1]

There are three points of particular interest in this definition. First, information can be received by any of the senses we possess. Although we traditionally think of information transference being accomplished by the senses of sight or hearing, other senses such as touch or smell may be equally effective. This will certainly come as no surprise to workshop practitioners, who frequently find it necessary to employ these methods for effective information transference to blind or other disabled clients.

Secondly, this definition suggests that information is not necessarily the same as raw data, as raw data may not increase the state of knowledge of the information receiver until it has been evaluated, collated, compiled, or processed in some other manner in order to make it useful.

Finally, information may be one or *more* occurrences which carry messages. It is doubtful that any organization exemplifies this statement better than rehabilitation facilities, where numerous occurrences concerning how to perform a certain task (in the form of "sign" language, examples by demonstration, etc.) may be necessary to transfer information to a deaf or similarly afflicted client. The importance of this cannot be overemphasized if we accept the notion that information must "increase the state of knowledge."

Having established the importance of information to management, it is easy to understand why effective information transference (vis-à-vis an MIS) is both desirable and necessary.

"A management information system is an organized method of providing past, present, and projected information relating to internal operations and external intelligence. It suggests the planning, control, and operational function of an organization by furnishing uniform information in the proper time-frame to assist the decision maker."*

---

[1] J. G. Burch Jr. and F. R. Stater Jr., *Information Systems: Theory and Practice* (Santa Barbara, Hamilton Publishing Co., 1974), pp. 23-24.

*From "MIS Universe," Date Management, September 1970 in article by J. Deardon, "MIS is a Mirage," in F. W. McFarlan, R. L. Nolan, D. P. Norton, *Information Systems Administration* (New York, Holt, Rinehart, and Winston, 1973), p. 72.

Therefore, the MIS is a formally organized system, which is employed by the organization to provide accurate, timely information concerning internal and external situations. It is invaluable to the decision-making process.

MIS DESIGN AND DATA PROCESSING

Much discussion on designing an effective MIS is devoted to the application of data processing and/or other mechanized methods of information transference.† The advent of the electronic computer has indeed encouraged the design of information systems to become more sophisticated and complex. But, in so doing we often find that many managers become more involved with the tools of information system design than in the actual design problems themselves. Because of this situation, it is not uncommon to find a workshop manager making the following statement: "I never seem to get the right information at the right time. What we need is a computer to solve our information systems problems."

While the computer can provide solutions to many information problems, we often find that inappropriate information systems design is a more pervasive problem in itself. When this is the case, the installation of a computer may only magnify a highly undesirable situation.

INFORMATION SYSTEMS AND DECISION MAKING

We feel that the best approach to information systems design is one of a decision-making nature, which emphasizes the need of getting the desired information to the individual decision maker. This approach requires us to regard the data processing

---

† For information relating data processing to MIS the interested reader may refer to D. J. Cougar and R. W. Knapp, *Systems Analysis Techniques* (New York, John Wiley and Sons, 1974); W. House, *The Impact of Information Technology on Management Operations* (Princeton, Auerbach Publishers, 1971); or R. G. Murdick and J. E. Ross, *Information Systems for Modern Management* (Englewood Cliffs, Prentice-Hall, 1971).

unit as a tool rather than as a panacea for design problems. In addition, it forces us to consider the usefulness and desirability of proper design of the information system first.

Much like other elements of the input sub-environment information is received and processed. (See Fig. 12, page 78.) When information is processed by an individual or an organization in such a way as to achieve a desired end, we find this process internally consistent with the various decision-making approaches outlined in Chapter 7.

The actual degree of complexity in decision making appears to be a function of two dimensions: (1) familiarity with similar decisions in the past (experience) and (2) the decision maker's knowledge of the ends that are considered desirable by the organization. In other words, the complexity of the decision-making situation is a function of both the individual's experience with similar decisions which can be "generalized" to the present situation, and the individual's knowledge of the ends that the organization wishes to attain‡ (See Fig. 19).

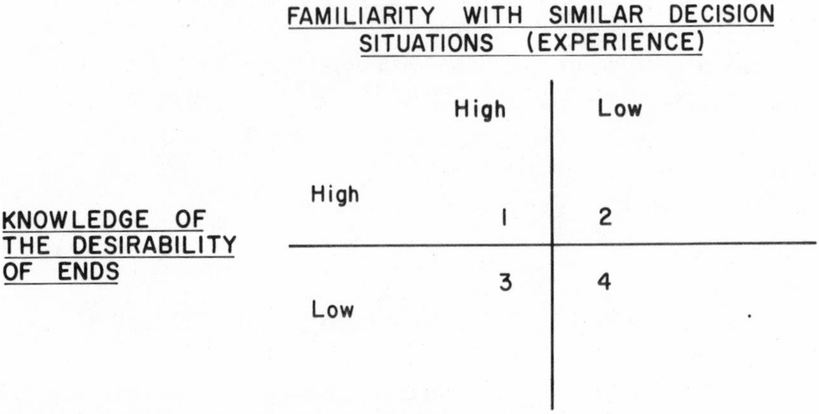

FAMILIARITY   WITH   SIMILAR   DECISION
SITUATIONS   (EXPERIENCE)

		High	Low
	High		
KNOWLEDGE OF THE DESIRABILITY OF ENDS		1	2
	Low	3	4

Figure 19. Complexity in Decision Making

In Cell 1, where both knowledge of the ends considered desirable and familiarity with similar decisions are high, we

---

‡Those readers familiar with J. D. Thompson, *Organizations in Action* (New York, McGraw-Hill, 1967), will realize our indebtedness to this author in our development of the dimensions of decision-making situations.

find decision making to be of a repetitive, routine, programmed nature.

A client responsible for repairing broken pallets, for example, will, upon finding a broken slat, remove it and replace it with a new one. If the client has been trained properly, the discovery of the broken slat will provide him with a situation with which he is familiar. Likewise, the knowledge of the organization goal (pallet reconstruction) should be reinforced with the decision becoming routine in nature.

Cell 2 presents a more complex situation which the decision maker might face. Here we find that though knowledge of ends desirable to the organization are high, experience with a similar or "generalizable" decision situation is low. If the individual (or group of individual decision makers) are interested in making a good decision, they will engage in what may be termed search activities.

This search may take various forms, from seeking other sources of advice, to gathering additional information. An executive director (who presumably has knowledge about what ends are considered desirable to achieve) may be faced with a decision with which he has had little or no past experience (for example, whether to change from a *mechanistic* management style to an *organic* style). Most likely our hypothetical executive director would channel his search efforts toward seeking additional advice from board members or other executive directors, or gathering more information from staff members or a management consultant.

In Cell 3 we find still another variation of complexity, with the decision maker's experience of similar situations high, with the knowledge of the ends considered desirable low.

A supervisor preparing paint for contract work may know (from experience) how to mix different colors, but unless information is conveyed to him by his superior as to how many items are to be painted in each color, he lacks the knowledge necessary to mix the proper amount. Again, we find that search behavior will be initiated, such as asking his superior how many items are to be painted, before the actual decision is made.

Finally, in Cell 4 (which is the most complex decision-making situation) neither the ends considered desirable, nor experience with similar decisions is available to the decision maker. While new staff members are frequently faced with this situation, the situation may occur with "old timers" too, particularly when the information system is inefficient.

Faced with this situation, the individual may: (1) engage in search procedures, (2) give up completely, or (3) pass the problem on to someone else. Although we would hope that most individuals face this situation only occasionally, repeated occurrences are likely to cause increased amounts of dysfunctional behavior (choices 2 and 3 above) and possible nervous conditions leading to extreme frustration and anxiety.

It is evident that as the decision-making situation becomes more complex, increased amounts of search are engaged in. These periods of search are time consuming and expensive, both to the individual (in maintaining his sanity) and to the organization (if they are interested in having the appropriate decision made). But, what causes the complexity of the decision-making situation to increase? (Can we, in effect, limit this complexity so that unnecessary search activities are eliminated?)

In answer to both questions, we feel that complexity of the decision-making situation increases because: (1) of increasing levels of "noise" in the communication process, (2) of differences in perception of the users, and (3) of design problems which occur as environments become more dynamic and technologies become more complex.

Although elimination of more complex decision-making situations can never be fully accomplished, it seems both logical and consistent that limits to complexity can be drawn if the decision maker is made aware of the ends that are considered desirable by the organization. This would, in effect, reduce a Cell 3 to a Cell 1, and a Cell 4 to a Cell 2 decision-making situation, respectively.

Since the desirability of ends are more likely to change with varying environmental and technological situations, we will concentrate on these areas in the remainder of this chapter.

ENVIRONMENTAL PENETRATION AND THE MIS STRUCTURE

It may be recalled from Chapter 9 that current empirical research indicates that different management styles are more effective under different levels of environmental penetration. The higher the level of penetration, the more effective is an organic style of management; while a mechanistic style of management is more effective under lower levels of penetration. We should expect then that the management style employed will have considerable impact on the MIS.

In situations where environmental penetration is high, there is a strong likelihood that "ends considered desirable by the organization" will change frequently. Because it becomes increasingly difficult under such situations for one or a few individuals to deal with *all* the environmental contingencies, we would expect that information would flow to lower and lower levels of management. We would also expect to find more information flowing across functional lines in order that the "desirability of ends" could be better determined.

On the other hand, with low levels of environmental penetration, we would expect to find a mechanistic management style where most of the strategic, long-range decisions are made only at the top management levels. Rules and standards of procedure would deal effectively with the repetitive, routine decisions that most of the middle managers would face in this environmental situation.

Therefore, it seems safe to assume that different management styles will, to a great extent, determine flow and content of information. While it is desirable under *any* management system to make the decision maker aware of "ends considered desirable by the organization," it is evident that in all but the top levels of management, the mechanistic system prescribes how these ends are to be met through "standards of procedures." In organic systems this is clearly not the case. This would seem to indicate that the bulk of information in a mechanistic system is of a procedural nature, while in an organic system it is of a decision implementing nature.

TECHNOLOGICAL INTERDEPENDENCIES AND THE MIS

In developing the concepts of the coordinative devices necessary under different types of technological interdependencies, J. D. Thompson supplies some valuable clues as to design priorities and the sophistication necessary in any particular MIS. In his schema he identifies three types of technological interdependencies: pooled, sequential, and reciprocal[2] (See Figure 20).

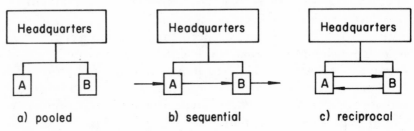

a) pooled   b) sequential   c) reciprocal

Figure 20. Types of Interdependence
(Taken from J. Galbraith, "Environmental and Technological Determinants of Organizational Design," in J. W. Lorsch and P. R. Lawrence, *Studies in Organizational Design* [Homewood, Irwin-Dorsey, 1970], pp. 113-139.)

Two units enjoy "pooled" interdependence when they share common resources from a common source but do not have any direct inputs from one to the other. For example, while two production units of a main workshop may share a common constraining resource (the total production budget), we may find that each of the units are in separate locations, with neither providing input into the other.

Sequential interdependence is more complex, in that the output of one unit becomes the input of another. Manufacturing firms employing long-linked technological processes (assembly lines) are the most familiar example of this situation, although as mentioned earlier, workshops may utilize this process in some varied forms (such as a sequentially arranged evaluation process).

---

[2] Thompson, *Organizations in Action*, pp. 54-56.

The final form of interdependence is termed reciprocal interdependence. When the output of one unit becomes the input of another and vice versa, reciprocal interdependence is being employed. We find that some vocationally-oriented workshops provide good examples of this form because of the high levels of reciprocal interdependence necessary between the rehabilitation unit and the production unit in trying to attain modification of behavior in a particular client.

COORDINATIVE DEVICES

In and by itself the identification of interdependencies is important, but for our purposes of even greater interest is Thompson's conceptualization of the different coordinative devices that prove to be effective as complexity increases (from pooled to reciprocal).

Under conditions of pooled interdependence, coordination by *standardization* is desirable. Since contact is minimal between the units and most situations that occur between the units are of repetitive, routine nature, rules and standards of procedure are most effective as a coordinative device. Since poorly devised procedures will provide unwanted headaches, care should be taken to ensure that procedures are appropriate to the situation.

The second type of coordinative device, *planning*, is more effective than standardization when dealing with non-repetitive situations. Where the scheduling of events is important, such as in sequential interdependence, planning is necessary in order that the flow of work is not held up. Most large client-centered systems employ intake and placement counselors who attempt to schedule their placements and "client intake" to coincide with each other in order to keep the system at full capacity.

The final coordinative device, *mutual adjustment*, is desirable when reciprocal interdependence is present. When one unit's output becomes the input of another and vice versa, increased levels of communication flow, feedback, and adjustment are necessary to accomplish coordination.

It should be evident that as complexity of the technological interdependence increases, the cost of noncoordination also increases. It should follow then that when consideration is given to design problems, priorities must be assigned to the resolution of the more complex information systems problems before the least complex of the interdependent situations (pooled) are considered.

SUMMARY

With the two previous chapters providing a background into technology and organizational structure, we feel that many of the conceptual design problems of MIS can be resolved by examining the level of environmental penetration and the complexity of the technological interdependence. When little penetration is present and the interdependence is not complex (pooled), we would expect to find *mechanistic* management styles more effective. Under this circumstance we would expect to find information flowing upward along functional lines because decision making is generally made at the top. Standardization of rules and procedures would generally prescribe the methods of decision making at all but the top management positions.

When, on the other hand, penetration is high or the interdependence between units require complex coordinative devices (mutual adjustment), we would expect to find information crossing functional lines (moving laterally) and decisions of a nonrepetitive nature being made at lower levels in the management hierarchy. This is so because the amount of information and decision making would be too great for any one individual to handle efficiently.

In this chapter, as in others, we've tried to provide the workshop manager with a conceptual view of some of the problems he is likely to face in the present. We would find it inconsistent with our approach not to extend these considerations to situations he may face in the future. In the following and final chapter we will attempt to predict and assess the complex forces which impact on the workshop. In our role as forecasters we are reminded of the story concerning a Polish visionary who claimed that he could see a synagogue burning to the ground in a town some forty-five miles away. Late the next day, a visitor from this rural hamlet appeared and discounted the seer's story. The local villagers were, however, still proud of their visionary: so *what* if he was wrong. Look how far he could see!§

---

§ Based on an account in W. G. Bennis, *Changing Organizations* (New York, McGraw-Hill, 1966) p. ix.

Chapter 12

WORKSHOP MANAGEMENT

AND THE FUTURE

I N ORDER FOR ANY conceptual framework to be truly useful, it
should provide not only for the analysis of current events
and situations, but also provide insight into the future.*
Strangely enough, much of the future of workshops is with us
today, if we only knew where to find it!

> If we knew where to look, we would find the future in our midst.
> The elements that will shape our lives in the next generation are
> already with us; the hardware and software of the future, the system of
> values, technologies, and business—all are among us in different
> stages of ripeness. Most of them are familiar and fully explored. It is
> from our understanding of these known systems whose basic proper-
> ties seem unlikely to change that we extrapolate for our understanding
> of the future.[1]

PERVASIVENESS OF CHANGE

If there is one theme which is dominant over all others in
describing conditions in the administrative world today, it is the
degree of change that is taking place. The theme of Alvin
Toffler's book *Future Shock*[2] (that change is occurring so swiftly
that individuals and organizations are overwhelmed by it) has

---

*It is interesting to note that different conceptual frameworks or paradigms have, at
various times, provided model problems and solutions for analysts. The development
and changing nature of paradigms is explored by T. S. Kuhn, *The Structure of Scientific
Revolutions* (University of Chicago Press, 1962).

[1] R. J. Roeber, *The Organization in a Changing Environment* (Reading, Addison-Wesley
Publishing Co., 1973), p. 1.

[2] A. Toffler, *Future Shock* (New York, Random House Inc., 1970).

never been a more telling description of the management situation than it is today. To this end, we feel it logical to examine some of the changes taking place in administrative and organizational processes in the workshop. In turn, this should provide us with the necessary insight to predict the future of workshops. Three areas of change are of particular interest. They include:

1. changes in management's assumption of the "nature of man;"
2. changes in the nature of the internal organization;
3. changes in the environment that the organization faces.

We will proceed next by examining each of these areas, with a view toward drawing some conclusions on the effect they are likely to have on workshop management in the future.

CHANGES IN MANAGEMENT'S ASSUMPTIONS OF THE "NATURE OF MAN"

In the first few chapters in this text, we examined the differences between traditional management thought, which viewed man as a machine, and the development of the behavioral school of thought, which emphasized the recognition of man's motives, needs, and values as a means toward understanding his motivation. This transition from the traditional to a behavioral philosophy was accomplished, for the most part, because of a change in management's assumptions about the "nature of man."

Edgar Schein has elaborated on these changes in assumptions by providing an interesting discussion of their historical appearance. In his scheme Schein identifies four varying assumptions about man: (1) rational-economic man, (2) social man, (3) self-actualizing man, and (4) complex man.†

---

†A complete analysis and implied managerial strategy for each of these assumptions may be found in E. H. Schein, *Organizational Psychology*, 2nd ed. (Englewood Cliffs, Prentice-Hall, Inc., 1970).

The first assumption about the "nature of man" views man as being rational-economic, meaning that he is primarily motivated by economic rewards. Since these rewards are distributed by the organization, man is under its control. Under this assumption, man is viewed as inherently lazy and as not sharing the goals set by the organization. An organization which accepts such assumptions will, of necessity, design itself in such a way that it controls (usually through coercion) man's unpredictable nature by establishing elaborate standards of procedure. These rules are to be followed by all but the top management personnel.

As indicated in Chapter 2, this early assumption of man's nature was felt far too inadequate to explain man's relationship with the organization. The Human Relationists felt man to be social in nature, motivated primarily through his social contacts and interactions with others. Under this assumption, other goals (principally of a social nature) were seen as being more important to man. Man would presumably respond to management to the degree that management helped facilitate his social needs. Finally, managers holding such assumptions about man naturally spent more time in group maintenance activities, as well as promoting the fulfillment of social needs.

More recently still, other behavioral scientists have agreed that these early assumptions about man and his relationship to his work are inadequate. A number of theorists (principally Maslow and Herzberg) are of the opinion that man is more interested in striving for self purpose and realization (see Ch. 3, page 24). Under this assumption, man is seen as being capable of accepting organizational goals provided that conditions of work are such that he can experience personal growth and self-actualization. Management's main purpose in this instance, is to provide interesting, challenging, and meaningful work for each individual.

Schein, while accepting some of the later tenets of behavioral science, felt that each of the three preceding assumptions of man were tautologically simple and unrealistic. To Schein, man's behavior was infinitely more complex than the expression of any one need.

> Man is a more complex individual than rational-economic, social, or
> self-actualizing man. Not only is he more complex within himself,
> being possessed of many needs and potentials, but he is also likely to
> differ from his neighbor in patterns of his own complexity.[3]

Therefore, assumptions of complex man view him as a highly complex, variable, individual whose motives are likely to change over time. At certain times with certain economic rewards, man may appear to be rational-economic; while at other times, social needs and rewards may be more important to him. Combinations and permutations of rational-economic, social, and self-actualizing behaviors are not only possible, but highly likely under these assumptions. If one adopts these assumptions, the manager's main task is seen to be diagnostic in nature, with the careful identification of individual needs as the primary step in successful accommodation of organizational goals and individual satisfaction.

THE NATURE OF MAN AND THE FUTURE OF WORKSHOPS

Even though Schein presents these assumptions of the nature of man on a historical continuum, it is evident from observations developed in this text that various workshop managers may hold any (or all) or a variety of beliefs regarding man's nature. We would hope that as workshops increase in complexity and sophistication, the complex nature of man paradigm would attract more adherents. Assuming this to be the case, the most relevant question would appear to be what implications does acceptance of this philosophy hold for the workshop?

Undoubtedly, new technologies for processing clients will be utilized. As indicated in Chapter 10, when "knowledge of the client" is low (and each client is therefore viewed as complex), unit processing technology is likely to be utilized more frequently.

With the increased utilization of unit technology, there will be a greater need for professional staff, as development of

---

[3] Schein, *Organizational Psychology*, 2nd ed., pp. 69-70.

custom-designed programs for each individual will be a necessary requisite. This increase in professionalism will be required to ensure that both the rehabilitative and managerial processes are considered jointly in assessing the effectiveness of the workshop.

Finally, increased networks of communications (between the rehabilitative and managerial disciplines) will become necessary in order to design and implement custom programs for each client.

CHANGES IN THE NATURE OF THE INTERNAL ORGANIZATION

Accompanying many of the changes already alluded to will be changes in the internal workshop organization. Organizational structure, technological complexity, and management styles will all be subject to change.

Although situational analysis will continue to be necessary in the determination of an appropriate structure; suffice it to say that as environmental penetration increases, we should expect to find more workshops employing *project* or *matrix* structural components as opposed to *functional* components. The reason for this is that project or matrix teams (combinations of functional and cross-functional elements to perform a given task) are usually more effective in dynamic environments.

Technologies employed in the future are likely to vary in both content and form. As regards content, it seems logical to assume that if the "nature of man" is considered to be complex, workshops will take on many characteristics bordering on the "intensive" as opposed to "mediating" technological systems. With such a change, the need for additional specialized skills and services should intensify. This will become necessary in order to properly diagnose client's needs and design programs to meet them.

Form (or structure) of technological systems seem likely to increase in complexity of interdependence. Since greater coordination between rehabilitative and management processes will be necessary to effect positive behavior modifications in clients, we would expect to find greater amounts of reciprocal interdependence among workshop units. Mutual adjustment as a form of coordination should be the prevailing method to accomplish this goal.

Inherent in these changes in technological content and form will be a markedly greater role for the client in various workshop processes. This will necessitate a much higher degree of communication and planning expertise. In order to accomplish this end, we feel that more and more workshops will move toward organic styles of management with the attendant cross-functional information flow. Whereas in the past, where decision making occurred only at the top levels of the organization, new and emerging internal and external conditions may point the way for increased participation at lower management levels, largely consisting of group decision-making processes.

CHANGES IN THE WORKSHOP ENVIRONMENT

Possibly the greatest change that will affect workshops in the future will take place in the environments they face. It is safe to assume that as changes occur at increasingly faster rates, the amount of environmental penetration will also increase. Subenvironments which can be expected to be particularly critical to the success of workshops in the future will include the governmental sector, the client system, and the community at large.

The government sub-environment, composed principally of regulatory agencies, service agencies, and legislative bodies have had, and will continue to exert increasing influence on the activities of the workshop. Priorities set by these agencies and bodies will place considerable importance on adhering to sound budgetary practices in workshops. New directions and changes of emphasis arising from these priorities will force workshop personnel at all levels to be innovative and imaginative with respect to program design. Finally minimum requirements set by these agencies will, in many cases, affect the structure and composition of workshop staffs.

Although many workshops still feel that their primary function is to provide a client with the skills necessary to acquire and hold a job in the community, it seems likely that in the future, workshops will become more and more involved with other aspects of client needs. Total rehabilitative facilities, with the fusion of many different areas of specialization seem likely to be the expanded version of the present-day workshop. These facilities would provide medical examinations, initiate social functions, and provide extended care services for those in need of such services during training, etc., and in general would provide all of the special services that smaller workshops are unable to provide because they lack "economies of scale." We are not suggesting, however, that all of the smaller workshops will disappear, because sophistication of this type (increased services) is not necessarily a function of workshop size. For example, a small workshop may provide these expanded services in cooperation with other local agencies.

Even though community support (in the form of donations) and guidance (in the form of voluntary participation on the board of directors) have always been a part of the workshop experience, we feel that this sub-environmental force will become much more crucial in the future. Legitimacy (sanctioning of the workshop by the community) will become increasingly important to facility managers as questions are raised about the methods and procedures utilized in the workshop.

This subsequent increase in environmental penetration will persistently dictate changes in the workshop's future. Since changes in management's assumptions about the "nature of man," changes in the internal nature of organization, and changes in the environment faced by the workshops are all closely interrelated, we would expect solutions to the problems of change to be multifaceted in character. For example, as environmental penetration increases, we would expect more workshops to employ organic management styles, emphasize greater communication flow, and encourage lower level decision making, to the extent that the individual possesses the information necessary to make the decision.

STRATEGIES FOR DEALING WITH THE FUTURE

Faced with the ever increasing amounts of uncertainty that accompany changes which are likely to occur in the future, workshops will surely court disaster if they are not prepared. We feel that the utilization of three strategies could be particularly helpful in dealing with changes in the future. They include: (1) increasing the professionalism of staff personnel, (2) utilizing a systems approach for analysis of problems, and (3) improving the diagnostic abilities of the staff members.

It should be evident that if we are to deal with the complexity of changes in the future, it would be highly desirable to deal on a conceptual level. As change increases in intensity, it is highly likely that the professional that possesses the skill and ability to conceptualize situations will be able to make the decisions considered to be in the best interest of the client and the workshop.

In examining the situations he is faced with, the professional should also find increased value in utilizing a systems approach for analysis.

> Systems examination—(is) looking at the organization as a complex, human system with a unique character, its own culture and value system. This character, the culture, and the values, as well as the information systems and work procedures must be continually examined, analyzed and improved if optimum productivity and motivation are to result.[4]

In other words, the systems approach is helpful because it requires the analyst to consider the consequences of his actions in *all* elements of the interrelated system. This requirement forces the manager to anticipate the depth and breadth of his actions before he takes them. Therefore, we feel that this approach has great promise not only when used in organizational system analysis, but also in group and individual (behavior modification) process analysis prior to implementing change actions.

---

[4]R. Beckhard, *Organizational Development: Strategies and Models* (Reading, Addison-Wesley Publishing Co., 1969).

Finally, since change will continue at an ever increasing rate, continued education and training are necessary in order to improve the diagnostic abilities of practitioners. In order to make the proper analysis of the situation, each staff member must be given the best analytic tools which are available. Equipped with these tools, the rehabilitation counselor may discover the underlying needs, motives, and values of his client in order to better motivate him, just as the workshop manager equipped with such tools may better determine the appropriate structure, information system, and management style.

In order to achieve a more acute diagnostic ability, the practioner must be exposed to a broader background in the administrative processes so that he may better understand how he can construct a more successful workshop. We hope that this book lays the foundation for such an effort.

NAME INDEX

SUBJECT INDEX

125